The Resurrection Mantra

Build hope and resilience into your life

By

John Moran

Preferential Publications Pty Ltd
Brisbane, Australia
contact@prefpub.com
www.prefpub.com

First published 2019

Copyright © John Michael Moran 2019
All rights reserved.

ISBN-13: 978-0-6485941-1-6

 A catalogue record for this book is available from the National Library of Australia

Preface

I BELIEVE there is a desperate and growing need for this type of book in the early 21st century.

There is a lot of unnecessary unhappiness, discontent, bitterness and loneliness in the world.

Great Britain was so concerned about loneliness levels it appointed a Minister for Loneliness in 2018. By 2019, deaths in the United States of America from opioid overdoses had reached epidemic levels, exceeding 45,000 annually, and that was only a fraction of the addiction levels. In Australia in 2019, with a population of about 25 million, it was estimated three million people — one in every eight people including children — were reliant on antidepressants and phrases like "medicating disappointment" started appearing.

I have worked for decades in issues management, public policy and media. During that time I have ploughed through countless market research, government, non-government organisation (NGO) and think-tank reports on the full range of human needs and services. For a number of years I also worked in pastoral care and educational settings.

Much human suffering and distress is unnecessary and the result of an excessive confidence in and reliance on so-called human progress, social science and political, medical and legal solutions. For most of my life I shared that naïve confidence.

After years of closely observing these options, it is clear they are inadequate, on their own, in helping us live happy, meaningful lives and maintaining a positive, hopeful outlook.

Large sections of the population in many countries are duped into believing the natural and social scientists and government programs - human effort and human reason - can solve all our problems, including our deeply personal problems. It is the great lie and the negative personal and social consequences of this mass delusion are increasingly evident.

Restoring simple spiritual exercises to the people will go a long way to dealing with the unnecessary mental anguish, which is now so prevalent.

To believe life is some perfect journey, where we can remove or avoid suffering, is a folly. But, to let life's setbacks undermine our lives and positive worldview is an even bigger folly.

John Moran
Brisbane, Australia

Acknowledgements

I would like to thank the following people for their advice and assistance:

Paula O'Dea
Professor Rachel Fulton Brown, University of Chicago, USA
Professor Janice Fiamengo, University of Ottawa, Canada
Peter Moran
Michael Moran

Contents

Introduction 1
Part One: Designing a mantra 5
    What happened to grandma's Rosary beads? 7
    The spirit is weakened 11
    Myself and the inner self 17
    Why does it matter? Suffering and hope 21
Part Two: Understanding and using the Resurrection Mantra 25
    An integrated life: Body, Mind & Spirit 27
    The Easter story: The basis of the Resurrection Mantra 31
    Evidence for the life-death-new life pattern 44
    The Resurrection Mantra and mantra exercises 56
    The Resurrection Mantra and life 67
    The Resurrection Mantra in eight easy steps 76
Postscript: Going a little deeper - John Cassian & Abbot Isaac 79
Post postscript: The bodily resurrection of Jesus Christ - A few thoughts for people of faith 83
Further reading 87

Introduction

PEOPLE around the world are gradually reawakening to the need for a spiritual balance in life. They are looking for realistic spiritual exercises, described in plain practical language, which help re-establish meaning in our lives and make sense of any suffering we experience or are fearful of experiencing. The solution is actually hidden in plain sight and has been a central cultural-religious theme in many parts of the world for approximately 2000 years.

This book outlines such a simple, practical spiritual exercise based on the fundamental rhythm of (and truth about) life: The constant flow of death events – setbacks, tragedies, losses - that side-track or disrupt our lives and whether they lead us to a living hell (despair) or resurrection (new life).

It is a personally developed and tested exercise that has worked for me, which might also work for you. That's basically it. Nothing complicated, but it can profoundly change your outlook on and approach to life, no matter what setbacks you experience.

It focuses on the life truth and the outcome options, summarised so clearly in the powerful story of Easter - the death and resurrection of Jesus Christ – which is the supreme example from history of life's life-death–new life pattern.

I developed and trialled this mantra exercise, involving a short phrase or (for people of faith) prayer, over the last 10 to 15 years. The phrase at the centre of the exercise - ***Jesus, with you I will die and rise again*** – was designed to embed this essential life-death-new life truth in my consciousness and train my thinking and temperament for when trials and tribulations come along.

Whether you are a Christian or not, whether you believe in life after death or not, the Easter story still describes the inherent potential of the many Good Friday events we go through on this side of the grave. The Easter story is not some obscure spiritual guru's thought bubble. It has been prominent in European culture for more than 1500 years.

It has been prominent in other societies for hundreds of years too. Easter is a holiday in many countries. For the Christian it reveals important truths about God and life after death. For everyone, it illustrates an important truth about life here and now.

In the words of the best-selling Canadian clinical psychologist, Jordan Peterson:

> *The idea of the death and resurrection has a psychological meaning, in addition to its metaphysical and religious significance. It can be thought of as part of the structure of narrative that sits at the basis of our culture. It includes elements of sacrifice (associated with delay of gratification and the discovery of the future) and psychological transformation (as movement forward in life often requires the death of something old and the birth of something new). (Source: https://www.youtube.com/watch?v=xPIanlF6IwM)*

According to the celebrated British writer, the late JRR Tolkien, it is the true myth.

The challenge is to internalise this truth, not just accept it theoretically. Thus, the Resurrection Mantra: ***Jesus, with you I will die and rise again.***

This Resurrection Mantra is, so far, changing my outlook on and approach to life significantly. I say "so far" because this story is about coming to terms with that basic truth: That our lives involve managing and getting through regular irritations, setbacks and, at times, catastrophes – "death" experiences.

If I am trying to be honest about life, it is important to be honest with you. The topic is not trivial. It is serious. As stated, it is about dealing or coping with life's difficulties, trauma, tragedy, suffering, pain, evil, cruelty, malice and catastrophe.

As I write this my life is obviously not over and I cannot speak with absolute certainty for the future. Although, this spiritual exercise is about preparation for facing the future meaningfully and positively, irrespective of what obstacles or catastrophes life throws at me. I would be surprised if it did not continue to assist me in the ways outlined. The point is, so far, so good.

It is not a self-help book. It is not a philosophy or theology book. Although it must dabble in those themes to some extent. It is not about lots of words, complex ideas or mysterious spiritual concepts. It describes a new spiritual exercise and simple, effective spirituality does not require such impenetrability.

Finally, it is not about avoiding or denying the reality of grief, hurt or stress. Anything but. That would be ridiculous and unrealistic; romanticism; a denial of human nature. The Resurrection Mantra is about the reality of life, not denying the way life is.

It is normal and okay to be angry, upset, depressed, feeling hopeless in response to an adverse life event, but it is not good for that to entrench itself as a permanent feature of your life.

It is about going through those legitimate responses to setbacks, trauma and catastrophe, without letting them drive you down the road of permanent despair. As you grieve and struggle, you still need and are entitled to hope. That is what a strengthened spiritual life - one based on the revealed and observable patterns of life and not wishful thinking - brings to such situations. (This integration of the Resurrection Mantra with the normal and legitimate emotional responses to loss and trauma is discussed in greater detail in Chapter Nine.)

In summary, this book is a story about a simple, personal spiritual exercise, which has helped me better understand and deal with an important reality of life – its life-death-new life pattern - which might assist you to do the same.

Part One

Designing a mantra

Note on Part One

Part One is not essential to using the Resurrection Mantra spiritual exercise. For those interested, it summarises how and why I developed it and summarises some relevant theoretical background and personal experiences and observations. If you wish to skip or delay this section and get straight to the Resurrection Mantra then go to Part Two and Chapter Five.

Chapter One

What happened to grandma's Rosary beads?

ONE THING I always looked forward to as a child in the early 1960s was visiting my mother's mother and father, my maternal grandmother and grandfather. It was fun visiting them. They were happy, generous people. They loved my brother and me very much.

My grandfather, from Cork in Ireland, was a humorous man and good story teller. He usually had a small gift for the two of us, maybe a coin for buying lollies, an ice cream he picked up on his way home or a toy he bought out on the road (he was a travelling salesman). My grandmother was an excellent cook and baker and homemade biscuits, scones and cakes were plentiful. Simple childhood treats were always awaiting our arrival. Her roast dinners and homemade desserts were special. And staying overnight? Well, that was just the ultimate visit.

There are happy memories aplenty, but in this context there is one quite different memory that, for some unknown reason, I still retain. Having said that, for most of my life, while I remembered the incident I did not think about its import or meaning much. That has changed in recent years.

The particular event occurred on one of those overnight stays I loved so much. I do not recall exactly how old I was, but it could only have been three or four because my brother and I were sleeping in our grandmother's room. I was lying there still awake and could hear her whispering on the other side of the bed. That was strange, as I could not see or sense anyone else in the room. There was no other voice. I broke my silence and demanded to know who she was talking to. I am saying my prayers, came the short reply in a low voice. Sure enough, I looked across to see her fumbling beads and mumbling; no doubt praying the Catholic Rosary.

It was my introduction to spirituality and, looking back, it was clearly an understated, but essential part of her life. No doubt it also contributed to her contented, unflappable nature. This was not "kneeling beside the bed prayer." It was not a chore or pious public display. There were no "prayer hands." It was day's end, with her comfortable in bed, quietly and privately focusing her mind and heart via the repetition of sacred words.

About this time I also became aware she attended morning Mass daily, not just on Sundays. She lived five or six houses from her parish church and took advantage of the convenience. Whatever else happened in her "Body" and "Mind" world throughout the day, here, at least, was a woman whose day started and ended with a spiritual exercise.

It was simple, unobtrusive and personal. She did not talk about religion or faith issues. She had the usual Catholic art and statues, but not too much. It was mostly in her own bedroom and on her dressing table. Visitors were not bombarded with it around the rest of the house. However, her Christian faith and its spiritual exercises were obviously the organising principle of her life.

It was not as if she had an event free life. She nursed both her parents at home until their respective deaths and also lost a child, her eldest son and an uncle I never knew, who died at home in 1945. During the prime of her life the world was at war twice. She had five other children to raise as well, while her husband was constantly on the road trying to sell milking machines, tractors and steam rollers. My mother, aunts and uncles were born between 1925 and 1935, the time of The Great Depression. There was no, "Why would I bring a child into a world like this?"

That first encounter with spiritual practice was about 1962-63. Many people my age in Australia, New Zealand, Europe and the Americas would recall at least one similar childhood experience.

In the years since, the world has changed significantly. In those 50 to 60 years, especially in large parts of what is often called the "western world," such spiritual practices are no longer as common as they were. Having lived through that time I am convinced people, in general, are not as content and settled as people like my grandmother were. I have observed a substantial change. The world as a place of risk, tragedy and evil has not changed, but how people respond to that reality has changed.

This is not some nostalgia for the so-called "good old days." It is an observation that something has happened, which is no longer taking into account an important truth about life and an essential aspect of human nature. Of course it is not universal, but there is now widespread neglect of the spiritual dimension of being human and the consequences can be seen everywhere.

For example, research project after research project points to growing levels of anxiety, stress, loneliness, drug abuse, frustration, fear and insecurity. I sense the research is right. My professional experience over the last 30 years, as an issues management and media adviser, also confirms it. I get similar feedback from most people I interact with, both in my own environment and around the world.

It is trite to pretend we don't have a spiritual dimension and that we don't need to take care of it and nourish it. One of the most easily-observable facts, for which there is evidence everywhere you look, is that there is a spiritual/religious dimension to human existence. Yet many cultures now try to deny or ignore the fact. That is risky for individuals and society. The decline of simple, uncomplicated spiritual exercises, like that engaged in by my grandmother that night nearly 60 years ago, is impacting negatively across society and in so many lives.

Popular psychology, thoughts for the day and self-help books and groups can be useful, but are no substitute for the resilience and wisdom, so evident in my grandmother, that goes with an integrated physical and spiritual life. This is not about mysticism or religious fanaticism. It is about the balance in our lives and the growing maturity that goes with accepting the truth that life involves a constant flow of challenges, setbacks and loss – "death" experiences.

The downgrading of spirituality's role in life is not new. It has been a work in progress, at least since the 1700s or what is usually called the Enlightenment. However, it was often an intellectual attack that did not fully engage the general public who, behind closed doors, maintained their beliefs and practices. The current situation is different.

People like my grandmother were commonplace up until the 1960s and 1970s, even into the 1980s. They are now an endangered species in many societies where they were once plentiful. What has happened?

Chapter Two

The spirit is weakened

Social and religious change

As I was first encountering my grandmother's spiritual life as a child, one of the great social revolutions of history was getting underway. To paraphrase the United States singer-song writer, Bob Dylan, at the time: The times they were definitely changing.

During the 1960s societies across the world witnessed social upheaval that is still cascading through those societies in the 21st century. That upheaval coincided with extensive change in the global organisation that was the spiritual backbone of Europe for more than 1500 years – the Catholic Church. The Second Vatican Council (a meeting of worldwide Catholic bishops held to discuss and regulate matters of church doctrine, discipline and practice) ran from 1962 to 1965 and by the end of the 1960s its decisions had ushered in a Catholic Church that many of its adherents at the time, such as my grandmother, did not recognise. This is not remembered by many in the 21st century, but it was momentous for those living through it. It fed into the other social changes then underway. Other churches and religions, though not all, also went through significant change at this time and in the years that followed.

A positive, optimistic enthusiasm characterised much of the energy unleashed at that time. Concepts like liberation and universal love and peace were amongst the objectives. Lots of good ideas and reforms emerged. However, every coin has a head and a tail and one downside was a widespread loss of spiritual practice and resilience in people's lives.

The social and religious changes, often supercharged with optimism, tended to gloss over or intellectualise the challenge suffering and setbacks presented at the individual level and ignore the need for simple, practical exercises, which developed and maintained a mature spiritual life. The consequences of that shift are now widespread. Growing numbers of people are looking to restore the balance with simple practices like those that sustained positive, tranquil people like my grandmother, despite whatever disappointments, setbacks and injustices life threw at them.

Media and advertising

Another aspect of life transformed since the 1960s is the media and information flow around the world. As an issues management and media adviser for about half of this period I have seen first-hand, and even done my own little bit to facilitate, that transition. Television and then the Internet have driven the change and the impact on people and society is significant. In the short term, at least, this has been subversive and even reached the point where the media is now frequently disrupting itself amidst falling audiences. Phrases such as "fake news" have become popular.

Anyone who looks at news articles in general newspapers up until the 1960s and 1970s and then compares them with headlines and articles in the 21st century will notice the difference. Most people are unaware there is a list of criteria known as "news values," which governs what journalists and newsrooms look for in a story. These include impact, timeliness, prominence, proximity, the bizarre, conflict, currency (is it trending) and human interest. A quick scan of this list and it is readily apparent why news content often portrays a skewed view of reality. So much is framed for dramatic and visual impact, rather than information provision, and to highlight points of conflict rather than agreement. Revenge rhetoric and hysteria get plenty of media space, while coverage of healing, resilience and perseverance is less frequent.

The pressure to win market share and be first with the news has frequently pushed the media into hyperbole, increasingly pronounced imagery and language and, occasionally, even serious error. Standard problems or issues become a "crisis." A handful of people with placards are a "community backlash." The need for television to have "colour and movement," rather than "talking heads," has led to exaggerated, bizarre and confrontational behaviour before the cameras just to get coverage. The instant nature of social media and Internet distribution has aggravated the problem. Media management and public relations have become a substantial industry, helping people and organisations exploit, manage and cope with the madness.

When conflict, disagreement, grievance and public humiliation become the measure of whether something is communicated to the public or not – that is, it is judged "newsworthy" - it is easy to see how people's perception of reality and their outlook on life can be distorted. If everything is a crisis or a failure or threat then why wouldn't you be anxious? If every past or present mistake or misdemeanour is an unforgivable sin, which can be paraded before a huge audience of friends and strangers alike, then it is hardly surprising many people's nerves are on edge.

Then there is the advent of low cost, high ratings reality television, such as arranged dating or marriage programs, strangers being locked together in a house for weeks with the cameras rolling all day and night and the combative "The Real Housewives of …" shows.

Operating hand in glove with this is advertising, the art of selling and market making. Advertising and promotion is not new, but since the advent of television and then social media, it has swamped most societies with its reach and influence. We are constantly confronted with its building of expectations and exploitation of our fears and dreams. It is relentless. No matter how hard you try you just cannot avoid it. Its methodology is based on twisting reality, manipulating perception and fantasy creation.

Most of these developments, especially since the 1960s, have descended into exploiting certain basic aspects of human nature and neglecting other key aspects, especially spirituality. Anyone who has ever worked in a marketing, advertising or campaign team in recent decades will confirm this. The market makers do not really want you to stop, centre yourself and think or reflect. If you do you are less likely to impulsively reach for your credit card.

Education and learning

Then there is compulsory, universal education, which became a feature of most societies in the late 1800s – only about 150 years ago. Given its powerful presence in the modern world it is easy to forget that it is a relatively new idea in human history. Since the 1960s there has been a continual expansion at both ends of childhood, with more, and more again, pre-school at a younger age and more, and more again, tertiary education at the young adult end. More children are starting formal classes at an earlier age and ending them at an older age, than in previous generations.

This has provided many benefits, but one risk is the creation of intellectual pride. The idea that you just need to learn more or acquire more information and it will all be okay, you will master the world and your place in it. Knowledge will solve everything. Science will conquer nature. This is the mass delivery of the rationalist delusion.

We are promised life without limit, health in perpetuity, psychological wholeness and wellness, the protection of group rights, protection of our bodies, unlimited career opportunities and prosperity for all. This is just another naïve utopia-building effort, which, upon close inspection, is not even close to realisation. Such a highly mechanistic view of the world and life is just another attempt to avoid reality. Unfortunately, for these latest utopia builders, reason alone does not provide all that the human person needs for full flourishing.

The skill is to take the many benefits a good education provides, while keeping imagination alive and developing your spiritual dimension in unison with improving the mind. Organisations like the Catholic Church established their own education systems to try and maintain this balance. Their effectiveness has slumped significantly since the upheavals of the 1960s and 1970s.

We talk about teaching children the "facts of life," but we don't. Real preparation for life – developing the spiritual resources to cope with the challenges and setbacks of adult life – is rare in schools. Despite the voluminous rhetoric about preparation for life, schools are basically career factories.

Material progress

Finally, there have been plenty of advances at the physical level, which have delivered more comfort and less extreme poverty. In many ways science and engineering have shifted us from a drab, hard world to a brighter, more comfortable world.

However, they have not necessarily delivered less stress. In fact, there is arguably more stress at the individual level. This is because poverty is relative. In a world of exuberance and excess, versus moderation and restraint, it is a comparison with those around us. Whatever environment we find ourselves in we are constantly operating within it as competitive actors. Every parent knows of the discord created if one child gets a bigger slice of cake or more drink in their cup than the other child.

The rational humanists like to point to economic statistics and claim things are so much better. In truth, it is not clear at the psychological and spiritual level. They are confusing physical comfort with personal peace or contentment.

Science and engineering have certainly made more and varied things. In many respects a world of things that swamps the senses: Bright lights, never ending messaging and signs, stuff everywhere.

It can be fascinating and distracting for a while. But, what happens when the novelty of the new wears off? Despite the popular joke about "retail therapy," consumption does not change catastrophe or malevolence or pain. So what then?

Reality versus utopia

We cannot resist trying to build impossible perfection or utopia. Many of the ideologies, or schemes and programs, which arise out of this flawed reading of human existence frequently take the place of religion or spirituality as a source of meaning for their adherents. They are distracting pipe dreams, a complete misreading of true human nature and aspiration.

The truth is, we can make the world better, in certain respects, but never perfect. The latter would not be progress, it would be a miracle. In reality, the solving of one problem often creates another one somewhere else, which in turn needs addressing.

In summary, the scientists and engineers can make existence more comfortable, but they cannot build us a future of undisturbed pleasure and freedom from responsibility. Nature does not work that way and, despite the crazy schemes and dreams of the utopians, we are bonded to the laws of nature. There is no escape.

Conclusion

These are some of the big changes that have impacted and continue to impact on us physically, psychologically and spiritually. There is constant talk about the effect of television, social media and computer usage on physical fitness and obesity levels. The fact is, they have had a more serious and potentially damaging impact on spiritual wellbeing for large numbers of people. Instead of thumbing Rosary or prayer beads everyone is thumbing the letters and numbers on their phone. Fitness centres are popping up everywhere, but churches, especially in the western world, are struggling.

Unlike so many revolutions of the past, which tried to suppress human spirituality in the name of reason, science, materialism, the super race or the working class, this cultural revolution has worked its way successfully to the level of the individual and their behaviour better than those old political revolutions did. This information revolution has captured the imagination of billions, increasingly occupied our personal and private space and distracted many from attending properly to their physical and/or spiritual wellbeing. I include myself in that.

To better enjoy and get the most out of life more of us need to rebalance a little and reconnect, deep inside ourselves, with the simple truth that life can be a series of knocks and rebounds, as long as our disposition gives the rebounds a chance.

This Resurrection Mantra is helping me find the balance. Given its simplicity, it might help you do the same.

Chapter Three

Myself and the inner self

Solid start

The Resurrection Mantra grew out of decades of effort, experience and trial and error devoted to sorting this Body, Mind, Spirit complexity out in my own life. It was not all-consuming, but it was something I would privately return to from time to time to try and get a better handle on.

I was raised a Catholic and within Catholic culture. I was inducted into the sacraments, doing First Confession and First Holy Communion when I was in the second grade. I was sent to a Catholic high school in the early 1970s. For a couple of years in the late 1960s I also served as an altar boy, with other boys from the neighbourhood. There was a strong social and cultural dimension to it all, which was fine in its own way – a sense of community, belonging, a level of spiritual engagement. Like everyone else I "said the prayers," but it was not any deeper than that.

This was at the height of that period, described in the previous chapters, when the wider world was being transformed by the 1960s and the religious world, whether Catholic or not, by the changes in the global Catholic Church arising from the Second Vatican Council's decisions. When something as big and embedded in society as the Catholic Church changed, it affected everything around it too to some extent.

My first year at Catholic high school involved daily religious education classes, which were of a solid academic standard. We studied religious ideas and biblical texts just as we would study material in any other subject. We did units on The Acts of the Apostles and The Book of Job. We studied the sacraments and read a book called The Christian Gentleman. We took copious notes, did assignments and got a grade.

This was similar to the rigorous First Confession and First Holy Communion preparation classes I did in the second grade in 1965 (just as Vatican II was ending), when age appropriate, but still serious, ideas about sin, forgiveness and receiving Jesus in Communion were presented. Awe, reflection and respect were expected when in church. For this six year old there was definitely a sense of mystery, difference and otherness about it all.

Changes aplenty

That first high school year was 1971 and it was the one and only year of such academic rigour being applied to religious studies or Christian Doctrine. The following year, the Ninth Grade, things changed and the tone was set for the rest of my time at high school. Those Christian Doctrine lessons basically became general discussion sessions about life, social issues, politics and sex education.

I also stopped being an altar boy and did not go to church. A few years after leaving school I started attending church again and trying to take spirituality seriously. I took courses and went to plenty of lectures and prayer days. The romantic nature of the Christian story and social message is enticing, especially when you are young. But, at another level it was a struggle and, in truth, it was not working for me. By 1986 I had stopped attending church again. It was decades later before I worked out why.

At the time I assisted with a lot of good work, in a "love they neighbour" or social welfare sense, but I could not get the personal spirituality right. It was all talk, talk, talk. Social justice, social justice and more social justice. Vatican II this and Vatican II that. Youth Masses, even loud, crazy "rock" Masses, and I was as guilty as many others in thinking this type of "activity," "intellectualism" and "entertainment" were what it was now all about. There was so much noise and chatter, interminable meetings and seminars, and the Church constantly talking about itself.

For sure, there was always enough talk about prayer and how prayer held it all together. But, again it was so often just words. What did that mean? I just could not make it happen. It was a chore. Boring, ineffective.

In the euphoria of the new open, experimental age, books were pouring off the presses about prayer, but, frankly, they were often so much inflated piety and head-in-the-clouds stuff. I had a library containing many such books, but I still could not get it and do not believe many busy everyday people got it or any benefit from it either. Certain insiders like priests, ministers and religious might have, but for the majority the simple spirituality of people like my grandmother was being swamped by words, words and more words. Simple spiritual skills were lost across vast sections of the population, which in previous generations would have acquired or "absorbed" them.

I am a classic case study in what happened and I am just one of hundreds of millions, if not billions. I saw, up close, my grandmother using those skills, but they were never handed on to me as society underwent the massive changes described above. My observation is that the situation for the generations following me is even worse and the risks and negative consequences are becoming clearer. Body, Mind and Spirit are out of balance for so many of us, across all age groups, and the one most neglected is spirituality and that is, arguably, driving many of the problems with the other two, such as eating disorders.

At the community level, the bells and smells and mystery of my grandmother's generation were often replaced by the atmosphere of a concert, lecture or public meeting depending on who designed the church ceremony for that week.

I am convinced the tendency to turn church ceremonies into social encounters rather than spiritual experiences has contributed significantly to the decline and neglect of spirituality in many societies around the world. Church attendance has been in steep decline in many countries. For those looking for a solution, the social encounter is probably best left until after the ceremony. The strengthening of visual and auditory beauty and rhythm and the maintenance of a sense of special space within the church walls is also important.

Restore spirituality

Don't get me wrong, you need an intellectual dimension. Just as you need a physical dimension, social dimension and moral dimension. But, it is spirituality that holds it all together. An integrated life involves all the dimensions – physical, psychological and spiritual or Body, Mind and Spirit, if you like. In fact, if you find yourself struggling to keep your physical and psychological life under control you can invariably trace it back to an underdeveloped spiritual life.

All those people talking to me about the importance of prayer or the inner or spiritual life were right, but talk is seldom enough. Like sticking to a diet, for our physical well-being, it is easier said than done. It all just went nowhere with me at the time and I believe it is going nowhere with increasing numbers of people today. People are anxious and unsettled because of it.

Since the 1980s I had been aware of this concept of death and resurrection applying to life's events this side of the grave. I was introduced to it in a healing program for widowed and divorced people called the Beginning Experience, developed by a group of Catholics in the United States. It was a powerful program, open to all comers not just Catholics, and I saw its effectiveness in many lives. As a result of the Beginning Experience program people were building new lives after the death of a spouse or the death of their marriage.

The death-resurrection idea never really left me and in the mid-2000s I started to reflect on it again and experimenting with a simple mantra exercise based on the Easter imagery.

For a number of years now this Resurrection Mantra has helped me start addressing the challenge of spiritual balance. And, so far, it's working extremely well. Given its simplicity, it might do the same for you.

Chapter Four

Why does it matter?
Suffering and hope

Managing stress, discontent and despair:
Suffering defines the world

One of the reasons neglect of our spiritual needs can be so debilitating, even dangerous, is that suffering defines the world. This is despite the many advances human beings have made. This is because those advances can only mitigate or change the risks, setbacks and tragedies of life, they cannot remove risk, tragedy or evil.

We instinctively know this. We know that any number of things, from the minor to the catastrophic, could go wrong in our life at any time. Anyone's life can change in a heartbeat or instant. Despite the confidence and smiles we might show the world, in our own solitude we know this is something to factor in and contend with.

That is why it is true to say that suffering defines the world. It has many causes and takes many forms, but, whatever the cause or form, it is the thing we are fearful of, the thing we expend extensive resources trying to avoid and the thing that undermines the quality of our life. In serious cases it can completely alter and/or damage our life and the lives of the people we love and care about.

No matter how well we might be doing at a given point in our life, sadness and loss are potentially never far away. Despite our best efforts we can only control things to a certain extent. Disasters and malevolence are a fact of life. Worry is a regular unwanted visitor and a cause of considerable unhappiness.

Of course, life also has its good times, its high points, its pleasures, but it is the weakest link that defines the strength or capacity of the chain and times of suffering are the weak points in our lives. They are the experiences that can trap us and bog us down. Yet, so much is invested in pretending otherwise, trying to avoid this reality. That is a recipe for disaster, especially when that reality finally inserts itself into your life in a serious incident. The problem is, ignoring reality or complaining about reality does not change reality.

This is not about pessimism, doomsaying, defeatism or taking the enjoyment out of life. As you will see in the following chapters, it is anything but.

However, it is the necessary starting point. You cannot get the most out of life if you deny or try to avoid this fundamental reality of existence – suffering defines the world and its negative impact is magnified when spirituality is neglected or avoided.

How you think about and handle potential and actual upsets, difficulties, tragedies and losses determines the quality of your life. This includes the numerous micro-mishaps and frustrations that happen on a daily basis, right through to a major catastrophe or loss such as a financial collapse, marriage breakdown or death.

All such incidents are, in one way or another, a death experience, in the sense that something has died or been lost – whether it be health, a job, money, a relationship or, ultimately, a friend or loved one to actual death. Grief is normal and has to be gone through. Being upset, angry and/or depressed is okay when you have been hurt or experience loss, but it is not good if such normal initial reactions become a chronic presence in your life because despair has set in or taken over.

Spiritual maturity is the only solution to not letting such incidents control, undermine or even derail your outlook on life and the unique, good things – life giving things - you have to offer.

The choice: Despair or new life

In your life's journey, every negative incident is a fork in the road, presenting two options – the path to despair (a living hell) or the path to new life (resurrection). Which one you choose will affect your life significantly. It is a choice in the end and too many choose emotional destruction, bitterness, unhappiness and discontent.

The strength of your spiritual life will help determine which path you follow. Does your life stall, with you becoming chronically embittered and unhappy? Or, do you push through the pain and anguish to a new life?

Because, as sure as suffering defines life, it is also true that it does not have to have ultimate power over its quality and your disposition. The evidence for this will be discussed in the pages ahead, but for Christians this fact was revealed and confirmed in the death and resurrection of Jesus Christ.

However, the story is not only relevant to Christian believers. For people of goodwill still grappling with faith issues, the death and resurrection of Jesus Christ, which has been such a central story in many cultures for up to 2000 years, is the pre-eminent story describing life's "death-experience to new life" rhythm.

Understanding this intellectually or theoretically is one thing, and an important starting point, but it is not enough. The truth is meant to be known and embraced, not just known.

Its integration into your disposition or personality and outlook on life is a process, driven and supported by regular spiritual exercises focused on the reality. You need an intellectual understanding and acceptance of this truth, but its effectiveness requires spiritual reinforcement.

This Resurrection Mantra has helped me with this spiritual reinforcement. Given its simplicity, it might do the same for you.

Part Two

Understanding and using the Resurrection Mantra

Note on Part Two

In Part Two we get into the practical aspects of the Resurrection Mantra – its place in an integrated life, how it works, how to actually do the spiritual exercise and its potential impact in various life situations.

Chapter Five

An integrated life
Body, Mind & Spirit

AN INTEGRATED, balanced life requires being conscious of and taking care of our Body, Mind and Spirit. Except for a few hard-line secular extremists, materialists or atheists, this is generally acknowledged as self-evident by most people, even if they are not sure how to do it.

The three categories interact and operate in a feedback loop with each other. That is why an integrated life deals with all three.

In the last 100 to 150 years there have been significant improvements around the world in physical comfort, educational opportunity and psychological understanding. There also has been a significant decline, especially in what is often called the western world (western Europe, Australia-New Zealand and North America), in spiritual/religious practice. It has not gone to zero, but there is an undeniable decline and this has accelerated since the 1960s.

As a result there is little argument that the "western world" is in something of a moral and spiritual crisis – a crisis of meaning for increasing numbers of people. Again, it is not universal, but it is definitely more widespread than in previous generations.

For example, there is an explosion of grievance and victimhood discussion in the public sphere, rather than a discussion of gratitude, acceptance of reality, healing and forgiveness. Underdeveloped or neglected spirituality causes drift, dissatisfaction, chaos, resentment and/or despair. Exploding levels of loneliness and drug addiction are typical symptoms of the malaise.

Before outlining the simple spiritual exercise, which is the subject of this book and might help you rebuild or strengthen your spiritual life and keep some balance, let's briefly discuss what the three categories of Body, Mind and Spirit are.

Case study: To illustrate each, let's consider the case of Paul who has to attend a meeting at which Tom, whom he recently had a nasty disagreement with and has not seen since, will also be present.

Body: The physical

This one is fairly obvious. It is our physical reality and needs. Our Bodily presence, in space and time, made up of atoms, molecules, cells, tissues and organs, which needs food and drink and protection from disease and injury if it is to work properly.

Case study: Paul and Tom are in the room together, sitting around the meeting table where they can see and hear each other. Will Paul abuse Tom across the table or go over and confront him up close, or will he compose himself and stay polite? He is physically close enough to exercise a range of options. Which one he chooses brings his Mind into play.

Mind: The intellectual/psychological

This is our ability to learn things, retain that knowledge or memory, reflect upon events and devise responses. The life of the Mind is the way we think, consciously form concepts, understand the world and make sense of it. That is, it involves thinking, rationalising, and understanding life and the world around us.

The life of the Mind is an essential part of life, a beautiful tool that should be kept in good order and fit for use. When it is, it allows us to make conscious choices, which are beneficial for us and those around us – living a sane life based on reason.

Structured and accurate learning and accurately-understood experience are essential to the development of the Mind. For example, we learn how to meet our physical needs and strategies for interacting with others through behavioural habits such as politeness, enjoyable conversation, cooperation and effective service. Most self-help books – for example, how to make friends or how to get that job you really want - target the life of the Mind.

Case study: Despite his anxiety and internal feelings of anger, Paul knows that a public outburst or loss of self-control at the meeting will damage his reputation in front of the others present. He decides to behave as if nothing has happened between him and Tom. He forces himself to say hello to Tom and engage with him politely when necessary during the meeting. It is learned behaviour in a social setting. His Mind is exercising control in accordance with that learned behaviour. Yet, his inner feelings and thoughts about Tom, invisible to the wider group, are quite different. This good life of human conduct is not matched by the inner reality. He is being polite, but his heart is not in it.

Spirit: The spiritual/religious

This is the next level again. Spirituality transcends rational thought, analysis and processing, which are the life of the Mind.

Spirituality is the inner life, which helps us stay in touch with the reality about ourselves, the realities of life and being and builds the inner resources to live with those realities and respond to them positively and with meaning. It is sanctity as opposed to just sanity.

Spirituality is private, inner disposition or orientation, which cannot be shared with others directly or observed by others. The fruits of it are shared with others, but these "fruits" could just as easily be a learned behaviour controlled by the Mind.

A times we do Spiritual things together – in a group or community - such as Catholics at Mass. In fact, the Spiritual life is more easily fostered and maintained in a group or religious context. It has become a bit trendy to try to deny this, but it is no coincidence that the Spiritual decline in western societies has gone hand-in-hand with a decline in church attendance and religious commitment. However, even within the religious group, the Spiritual experience is personal. It is an individual, relational thing; a personal journey. For the person of faith, it is their personal relationship with God and no one else can have exactly the same relationship.

A good life of human conduct does not necessarily equal a good Spiritual life. You might just have been taught or learned good habits. The Spiritual life helps add authenticity and integrity to the good habits or behaviour.

That is, the Mind forces self-control for practical purposes, but it is less stressful when your feelings follow the Mind and you actually believe in the self-control or what you are doing. Over time the psychological or Mind response alone can be hard to sustain without the Spiritual back up – the sense of purpose and inner commitment or belief. Thus, the benefits of developing your Spiritual life, not just your learning or "life of the Mind."

The Spiritual life requires regular Spiritual exercises for its development and maintenance. The more those exercises are based on intellectual and physical reality, rather than wishful thinking and complicated practices, the better.

The Resurrection Mantra outlined in this book is one such exercise, which might help you develop and maintain a stronger Spiritual life.

Case study: Paul prepares himself for the encounter with Tom in this meeting by calming and focusing himself, with a mantra, prayer or breathing exercise, until nasty feelings directed at Tom disappear. Paul does not need his Mind to work overtime to control his physical behaviour, because internally he has aligned his feelings with what he knows is correct. His frame of mind is aligned with his Mind. He not only knows what to do, but does it without mixed or conflicted feelings swirling around inside him. This, of course, is less stressful that fighting against your feelings.

Chapter Six

The Easter story
The basis of the Resurrection Mantra

THE RESURRECTION Mantra is a simple spiritual exercise, designed to embed a key life truth – its life-death-new life rhythm - into your being, your disposition, your outlook on life.

To use the Resurrection Mantra, whether you are a person of faith or not, you need to first understand a few key features of the life of Jesus Christ, especially the traumatic, unsettling events at the end – what is usually called his Passion. The Resurrection Mantra is based on those events.

Jesus Christ is arguably the most famous person in world history. He was certainly the dominant idea in European or western culture for nearly 2000 years. One way or another, his life has touched the lives of billions.

For Christians he is much more than that. He is also the Son of God, the second person of a Trinitarian God, the Word made Flesh, the Redeemer of Mankind.

For people of other faiths and even no faith he is a great teacher, role model, prophet.

Jesus Christ did a lot of preaching and teaching, but the game changer was his followers' belief that he rose from the dead after his execution. This belief transformed the group and built the foundation for Christianity, which is one of the world's largest religions. Its central story is of the saving power of the death and resurrection of Jesus Christ.

Christian books devote considerable space to discussing the historical event and its divine, cosmic meaning.

But, the Easter experience is not just a standalone redemptive event. It is also a key part of ongoing revelation – that is, this is how life is. For the believer, God confirms this fact in his Son, Jesus Christ, at Easter.

That is, it is the archetype, or perfect example, for the life-death-new life flow of our lives. It precisely illustrates this deep and profound truth about life.

According to the popular Canadian clinical psychologist, Dr Jordan Peterson:

> *This is the diamond at the center of the world. ... This is the Great Truth. This is the responsibility whose acceptance allows each of us to live despite the catastrophic fragility of our limited being.*

As already stated, this is not a theology book. It is not a Bible study. Accounts of the death and resurrection of Jesus Christ are contained in the four Gospels in the Bible's New Testament. Reading the Gospel accounts will give you even greater insight into the Passion events. However, the Resurrection Mantra simply requires a familiarity with those events, not a chapter and verse knowledge of the Bible.

Imagery of the events is also plentiful in the art and film worlds and much can be located on the Internet. This material will also assist you understand and visualise what happened.

Finally, while we talk about examples or archetypes, when visualising what happened to Jesus Christ in Jerusalem during that first Easter, always remember that it happened in real, identifiable places, at an identified time and with real people involved. That sets it apart from so many other stories, myths, legends, proverbs and aphorisms we might be familiar with.

So, in summary, what did happen?

Lead up

1. The ministry years

Jesus Christ lived about 2000 years ago in the Middle East, in what is now Israel and Palestine. He was a Jew, born in a town called Bethlehem. At the time the area was under Roman Empire rule.

At about the age of 30 he set off on a preaching, teaching and healing tour around his homeland and gathered around him a committed group of followers. He also proved popular with the wider population. He spoke plainly and with authority and regularly gathered large crowds of simple people, who looked to him for help and claimed he freed them from ailments they had suffered under for years.

A lot of what he said and did was recorded in the four New Testament Gospels.

This went on for about three years until the resentment of some religious leaders led to his arrest and execution.

The beginning of the end

1. Palm Sunday: Entrance into Jerusalem

After three years on the road he decided to go to Jerusalem, where the Jewish Temple and the senior Jewish and Roman leaders were located.

The Jewish leaders were extremely nervous about him. Despite that, he was popular with the people and entered Jerusalem to great fanfare on the Sunday before the Passover, a Jewish festival that commemorates the Bible's Exodus story about the Jews' liberation from slavery in Egypt and their delivery to the Promised Land (modern Israel and Palestine).

So, his life was rolling along fairly well. He was popular and had lots of friends and people who loved him. However, he was also collecting a few enemies and people who resented him.

2. Incident in the Temple

Once inside Jerusalem he was still popular with the people and continued teaching and healing. This included daily services at the Temple. Some of the things Jesus said or insinuated, especially about them, angered the religious leaders.

On one occasion at the Temple Jesus became annoyed with the commercial activities being conducted in a holy, spiritual place – what should be a house of prayer and worship. He created a disruptive scene. The religious leaders were already annoyed enough, but this really upset them. He must be dealt with.

It was quite a mood swing. One minute it is palm waving, dancing and loud Hosannas, the next it is tension, anxiety and scapegoat hunting.

3. Betrayal

As part of the plans to stop Jesus, the religious leaders try to entice one of his closest friends – one of the Apostles - to betray him. They succeed in this strategy and the Apostle Judas turns on Jesus. At some point Jesus became aware of the betrayal and realises he is facing a crisis.

Death and Resurrection

1. Last Supper

At a meal, the Passover Meal, with the Apostles on Thursday evening Jesus tells them of the betrayal and the predicament he is now in. The Apostles insist they are with him and loyal. He goes out of his way to make the event a memorable one for them, using words and ritual they can remember him by.

2. Gethsemane

After the meal a distressed Jesus goes into a nearby garden – Gethsemane – to pray and restore his spiritual strength. He bargains with God to get out of the situation he finds himself in, but then accepts it is a given and nothing is going to change. His friends were so upset they fell asleep from exhaustion, and provided little support.

Judas, who had slipped out of the meal earlier, and the religious leaders then arrived to arrest him. His friends, the Apostles, wanted to defend him and fight back. Knowing it was of little use Jesus called for calm and went with the arresting party. Judas later committed suicide.

3. Custody and trial

The next day Jesus goes through a series of interrogations in front of the Jewish and Roman leaders, in which he maintains his composure and resolve. At one point a mob of onlookers taunts him and demands his execution. As Jesus predicted at the Passover Meal, one of his best friends, the Apostle Peter denies a number of times that he even knows Jesus. When Peter realises what he has done he is distraught with grief and shame.

4. Sentencing and execution

After a lot of toing and froing and people trying to pass the buck to each other, Jesus is condemned to death despite the Roman authorities being unable to prove anything against him. The accusations were enough. The injustice continued when the mob supported the release of a guilty man and demanded Jesus be killed instead.

The public humiliation and physical suffering then intensified, with whipping and a mock crown of sharp thorns pushed onto his head. He is then forced to carry the cross to the place of execution through a noisy crowd of onlookers, including some of his grieving female followers.

At the execution site the painful process of nailing him to the cross was conducted and the wooden frame with his body attached was then raised to the vertical position, with two other condemned men on either side of him. The soldiers continued to insult and mock him. His anguish was evident, but once he accepted the reality of his situation he restored his inner calm, even proclaiming words of forgiveness for his tormentors. Within a few hours he was dead.

5. Burial

Aware he was dead, some supporters asked the authorities if they could have the body for immediate burial before the Saturday Sabbath. After some negotiation and investigation they secured agreement and Jesus was buried in a rock tomb with a stone across the entrance.

6. Resurrection and New Life

On Sunday morning a number of female followers went to the tomb, which they found open and the body missing. There was a lot of uncertainty and scepticism, but eventually Jesus catches up with his followers who were stunned. His body still carries the wounds from the execution events, but everything has changed. The group has reached a new understanding, a new worldview. Despite the pain and suffering of the last few days, Jesus is transformed and so are the followers. Despite all the let down and confusion, relationships are rebuilt and even emerge stronger. They have a new sense of purpose. Their lives are changed forever. Death, suffering and grief have generated new life. Suffering and fear of suffering will never have the same hold over them again.

In fact, the group of followers is so transformed that they devote the rest of their lives to preaching about Jesus Christ and establishing Christianity in the face of great risk and constant persecution.

This is obviously an extreme event. Few life events are more terrifying, humiliating and painful than what happened to Jesus Christ. The Roman cross was a terrible instrument of torture. The prolonged physical suffering involved with crucifixion defies description. The psychological distress Jesus Christ experienced was also horrendous. He was abandoned, betrayed or denied by his friends. Onlookers mocked and taunted him.

This, of course, is the point. It is the key to the event's power. It is the great story from history about trust in the face of doom. No matter how bad things get, there is some type of new life at the other end of such processes.

While few will ever go through such an extreme event, there are aspects of it that feature in more common tragedies or malevolent events, such as:

- a life going along well, which is quickly upset by a crisis;
- mob accusations or gossip;

- public humiliation;
- physical pain;
- friends letting us down and even betraying and disowning us; and
- bargaining or pleading to get out of difficulties and avoid reality.

These are all familiar enough experiences for most of us.

Suffering is the result of evil, injustice and tragedy

Another reality illustrated in the treatment of Jesus Christ by the religious and Roman authorities is that suffering is caused by evil. This is a vital point. It is not to be glorified. Suffering is not a good thing. It is the result of tragedy, nastiness, incompetence, selfishness, greed. However, it is a fact of life.

You don't go looking for suffering just so you can experience some sort of new life. However, unfortunately, from time to time suffering will find you. There is nothing you can do about it.

Getting petulant and sullen about it will not make it go away or undo what has already happened.

Christianity itself, which arose out of the death and resurrection of Jesus Christ, is clear about this. Life is flawed and compromised by human evil and limitations. However, the death and resurrection of Jesus Christ illustrate there is a way through it.

Back in 1984, Pope John Paul II wrote a comprehensive letter to the people of the world, titled *Salvifici Doloris*, in which he made this clear:

> *Suffering happens, as we know, at different moments in life, it takes place in different ways, it assumes different dimensions; nevertheless, in whatever form, suffering seems to be, and is, almost inseparable from man's earthly existence.*

And:

> *...Christ in his Cross and Resurrection does not abolish temporal suffering from human life, nor free from suffering the whole historical dimension of human existence, it*

> *nevertheless throws a new light upon this dimension and upon every suffering...*

Significantly, John Paul II reaffirmed that Christianity proclaims the essential good of existence and the good of that which exists, acknowledges the goodness of the Creator and proclaims the good of creatures. However, "the reality of suffering is explained through evil":

> *Man suffers on account of evil, which is a certain lack, limitation or distortion of good. We could say that man suffers because of a good in which he does not share, from which in a certain sense he is cut off, or of which he has deprived himself. He particularly suffers when he ought—in the normal order of things—to have a share in this good and does not have it.*

In the midst of what constitutes the psychological form of suffering - pain, sadness, disappointment, discouragement or even despair - there is always an experience of evil, which causes the individual to suffer.

Professor Rachel Fulton Brown, at the University of Chicago's History School, provides a unique insight into just how evil and what an injustice the trial and crucifixion of Jesus Christ were. It is especially relevant in a world where cyber bullying and "gotcha" culture are causing so much suffering.

Professor Fulton Brown reminds us there is a reason to be afraid of the mob. The mob will kill you. The arrest, trial and crucifixion of Jesus teaches us this. The crucifixion of Jesus was a kind of lynching.

Jesus died because the authorities handed him over to the mob. Pilate washed his hands and the mob called for it.

Shame is the first step. We are dealing with real shame culture here. Once this is done you are allowed to punch them, you are allowed to kill them. This is a core human experience. If you can get a mob to declare against an individual – and it's often an individual; because if two mobs go after each other it is war.

This is why people don't often stand up to the mob. The experience of Jesus Christ shows you where it leads:

> *This is the worst sin of humanity. Why does Jesus have to die in the way that he does? Because he is expiating the most evil thing that human beings do together, which is band together in mobs to kill the innocent.* (John Moran and Rachel Fulton Brown, private communication.)

On the other hand, the death and resurrection dynamic pushes the boundaries of the experience of pain and suffering. You push through the limiting power of evil and malevolence and tragedy to new life. When these things catch up with you, which they will at various times of your life, it is all you can successfully do. Over time you cannot successfully run from the deep injustice, deep cruelty, deep hatred, pain and all the negativity of life without ending up in a rut of timidity, bitterness and/or despair.

So, suffering should not be glorified, evil should not be justified, bad things should not be glossed over and injustice is wrong. On the other hand they will happen and, if and when they do, you cannot make them unhappen.

JRR Tolkien & the true myth

For lovers of great literature, it is worth asking: What did *The Lord of the Rings* author, JRR Tolkien, have to say about the death and resurrection of Jesus Christ? The answer is helpful in the context of the Resurrection Mantra.

It is indisputable that Tolkien is one of the world's most treasured writers. Depending on which list you consult *The Lord of the Rings* is either, apart from books like the Bible, the first, second or third best-selling book of all time, at about 150 million copies. When joined with *The Hobbit*, at about 100 million sales, it makes Tolkien the only author to have two books in the top five or top ten, again depending on which list you consult, best-selling books of all time.

Those stratospheric sales numbers suggest Tolkien knew a thing or two about stories, storytelling, creativity, word pictures, mythology and levels of meaning. He used that knowledge to say a few perceptive and penetrating things about the death and resurrection of Jesus Christ – the true myth.

You see, Tolkien was a Catholic and you cannot understand JRR Tolkien or his great books unless you understand that. He believed he created because he was created. He told stories – in fact, we all tell stories – because God is a storyteller. In fact, God is *the* storyteller. We tell stories with words, but God tells stories with history – a theological word for that is revelation.

Thus, the great myths, which are not mere arbitrary inventions of fiction, have not been pulled out of thin air. Myths show us truth itself. Through story – a sub-created secondary world – they illustrate truths about the real or created primary world. The primary world is created by God. The secondary world is a sub-creation by man. Through myth, history (the primary world) and story (the secondary world) merge.

Such myths, according to the word's authentic definition, function as a worldview in story form. They contain an understanding of:

- How things are created
- What holds everything together
- Right and wrong
- How the world will end (sometimes).

In his famous essay *On Fairy Stories* – not fairy in the fairy tale sense, but Faërie or myth - Tolkien summarised the link with reality this way:

> *Probably every writer making a secondary world, a fantasy, every sub-creator, wishes in some measure to be a real maker, or hopes that he is drawing on reality: hopes that the peculiar quality of this secondary world (if not all the details) are derived from Reality, or are flowing into it.*

So eternal truths about the human condition can then be understood in ways that cannot be done by a sermon or technical book.

For Tolkien, the unrivalled storyteller, a key feature of such successful story telling is the happy ending - the sudden happy turn in a story that pierces you with joy. It:

> *...produces its peculiar effect because it is a sudden glimpse of Truth, your whole nature chained in material cause and effect, the chain of death, feels a sudden relief as if a major limb out of joint had suddenly snapped back. It perceives – if the story has literary 'truth' on the second plane (....) – that this is indeed how things really do work in the Great World for which our nature is made.*

He even invented his own word for it: Eucatastrophe - from the Greek ευ for "good" or "well" and καταστροφή for "disaster" or "catastrophe."

The "greatest eucatastrophe," or good catastrophe, was the death and resurrection of Jesus Christ, because it *"produces that essential emotion: Christian joy which produces tears because it is qualitatively so like sorrow, because it comes from those places where Joy and Sorrow are at one, reconciled."*

Jesus Christ is the underlying reality in which all the other stories have their source and the story to which all the other stories point. The resurrection was this underlying reality breaking into this world. Tolkien was clear, the story of Jesus Christ is not just a story, it is a true myth: a myth working on us in the same way as the others, but with this tremendous difference that it *really happened.*

Christianity is historical. Jesus Christ existed. So did Pontius Pilate. It is the true myth. The true story, the archetype. It is the true story that makes sense of all the other stories. For Tolkien all the bumbling efforts of man down the ages to blend history and story, through myth, are brought together in this one, mighty historical event:

> *I would venture to say that approaching the Christian Story from this direction, it has long been my feeling (a joyous feeling) that God redeemed the corrupt making-creatures, men, in a way fitting to this aspect, as to others, of their strange nature. The Gospels contain a fairy story, or a story of a larger kind which embraces all the essence of fairy-stories. They contain many marvels—peculiarly artistic, beautiful, and moving: "mythical" in their perfect, self-contained significance; and among the marvels is the greatest and most complete conceivable eucatastrophe. But this story has entered History and the primary world; the desire and aspiration of sub-creation has been raised to the fulfilment of Creation. The Birth of Christ is the eucatastrophe of Man's history. The Resurrection is the eucatastrophe of the story of the Incarnation. This story begins and ends in joy. It has pre-eminently the "inner consistency of reality." There is no tale ever told that men would rather find was true, and none which so many sceptical men have accepted as true on its own merits. For the Art of it has the supremely convincing tone of Primary Art, that is, of Creation. To reject it leads either to sadness or to wrath.*

So, there you have some of the reflections of one of the world's greatest storytellers on the greatest story ever told – the true myth about the life-death-new life rhythm of life, which is the basis of the Resurrection Mantra spiritual exercise.

In the next chapter we will look at how, as Tolkien said, it is the "story that makes sense of all the other stories" in your life. It is the "underlying reality" to which all the life-death-new life events in your life point.

Notes: JRR Tolkien, *On Fairy Stories,* http://heritagepodcast.com/wp-content/uploads/Tolkien-On-Fairy-Stories-subcreation.pdf; JRR Tolkien, *Letter*

89, Tolkien Gateway, http://tolkiengateway.net/wiki/Eucatastrophe; Tim Willard, *Eucatastrophe: J.R.R Tolkien & C.S. Lewis's Magic Formula for Hope*, A Pilgrim in Narnia, 2015, https://apilgriminnarnia.com/2015/12/21/eucatastrophe/; Lewis and Tolkien Debate Myths and Lies, *Tolkien's 'The Lord of the Rings:' A Catholic Worldview*, EWTN, https://www.youtube.com/watch?v=NzBT39gx-TE

Chapter Seven

Evidence for the life-death-new life pattern

EVERYONE, to some extent, can relate to the horror of the Easter story and identify with at least some of its phases – betrayal by friends, the pleading for help in Gethsemane, the nasty mob, the procession to Calvary, the pain of the crucifixion. The shock, humiliation and despair of Friday and Saturday.

The challenge is connecting, in a meaningful, lived way, to the idea that emergence on the other side, on the Sunday – new life – is also a part of the experience. The challenge is to avoid suffering and pain degenerating into the loss of meaning and purpose, to the conclusion that life is absurd and hardly worth living, let alone living positively and energetically. Such an outcome unnecessarily takes suffering to another level altogether, the level of despair or chronic bitterness and discontent.

Whether you are a Christian or not, the Easter story still describes the inherent potential of the painful Good Friday-type events we experience from time to time throughout our life.

How the Easter story describes the rhythm of life – life and death and new life - is confirmed in so many other aspects of life.

We can see the evidence, the pattern, everywhere at the individual and collective or group level.

This is an important step in the Resurrection Mantra spiritual exercise. It is not wishful thinking. It is not positive-thinking, popular psychology. It does not remove the pain or the stages of grief endured during the "death" segment of the process (we will talk more about that in the next chapters). However, it is observed reality. No matter what setbacks you experience there will be some sort of new life emerge if you choose to look for it, see it and embrace it: ***Jesus, with you I will die and rise again.***

The best-selling Canadian clinical psychologist, Dr Jordan Peterson, who has also published on this issue (On the Death and Resurrection: A Psychological View in Five Parts), agrees there is plentiful evidence for life-death-new life in the world.

Dr Peterson, with his extensive clinical experience, says we all see this death and resurrection pattern in our day-to-day lives, and we all know it, because we see it:

> *A small failure—a small disappointment, frustration, or disenchantment—engenders within us a small death, a small descent into the underworld, a small requirement for rebirth. A large failure produces a proportionately large catastrophe and transformation. When you are compelled to talk to someone because you face divorce, or the failure of a treasured ambition, or the illness or death of someone close, you are walking yourself through the eternal narrative: stability-crisis-death-transformation-rebirth. That's the story of our lives. That's the fall and the re-establishment of Paradise.*

He says that psychological progress—indeed, learning itself—requires continual death and rebirth, of lesser and greater magnitude:

> *If you are engaged in a serious interpersonal conflict or argument, or facing a true crisis in your life, the new information confronting you cannot be incorporated without the oh-so-painful demise of your previous conceptions.*

Now let's look at some of the evidence.

Examples

Examples – both individual and collective – of the life-death-resurrection pattern are easy enough to spot in the natural world. To our emotional and spiritual cost we often don't frame what we observe that way. In this section we will get into some of the nitty-gritty of life and help you see more clearly the life-death-new life pattern embedded in existence.

For humans the three dimensions of Body, Mind and Spirit are involved, and our choices and disposition or attitude are critical to the ultimate impact of "death" events or experiences.

The optimal rhythm of life-death-new life is often derailed or stalled because of our own approach to or outlook on life. There are many examples in our own lives and the lives of others of the successful transition through a death experience to new life. These can be after small setbacks or irritations all the way through to major crises.

There are no doubt also examples of unresolved incidents that are still eating away at us and holding us back.

There are far too many people whose lives are drifting, joyless or bogged down in bitterness and despair because of their reaction to the, real or perceived, harsh way life has treated them. In too many ways contemporary culture feeds this pessimistic narrative, rather than helping people develop the spiritual insight or maturity to break out of it.

Death events or experiences

A "death" event or experience is any irritation, setback, crisis or trauma – minor, middling or major – that involves loss.

From daily micro-aggressions through to life changing catastrophes we are constantly being confronted with "death" events or experiences.

Examples of such events include, in no particular order:

- Loss of an argument at work
- Rejection of an idea by others
- Being criticised by others
- Being ridiculed or attacked online
- Ruining your lunch
- Spilling your coffee
- The computer crashing
- Losing your wallet or purse

- Locking the keys in the car
- Locking yourself out of the house
- The electricity going off
- The car breaking down
- The bus, train or plane being late
- Unplanned pregnancy
- Emigration
- Forgetting to put the rubbish bin out
- A speeding ticket
- Burning your breakfast
- Being betrayed by a friend
- Parental desertion
- School bullying
- Missing a career promotion
- Not getting the grade or exam mark you wanted
- Missing out on the job you applied for
- Losing your job
- Losing a contract
- Breaking your arm or leg
- Breakup of an intimate relationship
- Separation or divorce
- Imprisonment
- Your pet dies or has to be euthanised
- Car damaged in a road accident
- House damaged or destroyed by fire or natural disaster
- A child is diagnosed with a serious illness
- A miscarriage
- A bad investment
- Marriage
- Being a crime victim
- Illness or injury
- Getting older
- Loss of a business

- Broken dreams, such as lifestyle, career, relationship and family aspirations
- Death of a child
- Death of partner
- Retirement

No doubt you can think of a lot more. The list is virtually endless, which is why life overwhelms so many people. Physical comfort and sensible intellectual/psychological skills can help manage things. However, it is spiritual maturity that keeps things in proper perspective.

Establishing that proper perspective involves categorising such events for what they are – death events, an event when something in us or around us dies. Let us look at a couple of examples to illustrate the point.

1. Being ridiculed or attacked online

Part of our privacy, self-confidence, public image and reputation dies. It is embarrassing and upsetting.

2. Locking the keys in the car

Control over the vehicle dies. Part of our daily schedule dies as time is lost fixing the problem.

3. Separation or divorce

A marriage dies. Love and respect dies. A whole list of dreams die – growing old together, enjoying the simplicity and efficiency of a happy family living together, providing the children with a unified, safe, secure environment.

4. Marriage

This is one not usually considered, but many marriages go through difficult periods at the start because marriage represents the death of the single, independent life and it is a shock for some people. One lifestyle has died and is replaced by another, quite different one. This can be a painful experience for certain people and, to make sense of it and better handle it, the experience should be seen as a life-death-new life event.

You die to the single life and rise to a new shared life. It can take time and involve physical, mental and spiritual adjustment.

5. Getting older

The death of youthful energy, dreams and idealism. Death of the "trim, taut and terrific" look of our teens and twenties. The death of clear, unwrinkled skin. Death of a decent head of hair or its unblemished colour. Dying eyesight. Dying libido (e.g. impotence) and reproductive function (e.g. menopause).

It is recommended you go through the list and even add to the list and then, for practice, itemise some of the things that might "die" to you in each case. Use this simple format:

Incident description: Losing a job

Things that partly or fully died: Financial security, loyalty ... (Can you think of a few more?)

Even the ones that might seem minor, can be annoying and destructive events when they happen regularly enough. Collectively, they can contribute to a "bad day" and personal frustration and kill your positive outlook and good mood.

Spouse 1: How was your day?

Spouse 2: Don't bring it up. So-and-so said something sarcastic about one of my proposals in a meeting this morning and I have been fuming all day. I could just tear strips off her and I might tomorrow.

The incident not only upset her all day, but now she has brought her agitation and bad mood home as well. It could even escalate into a more serious incident tomorrow.

Do not underestimate or dismiss this. In a workplace or other community setting little aggravations can combine to build a toxic interpersonal culture and low morale. They kill off the enjoyment of work or getting together.

Some people can fume for days over a little comment that they take personally or perceive as a slight. That is the death of their peace of mind.

In larger workplaces, human resource departments now exist to try and manage this type of thing. Currently, most people do not have the spiritual skills to keep these micro-aggressions in perspective. Even if they do have some spiritual skills, they often don't see these minor incidents as death events, but they are.

To maintain your composure and contentment in the face of the constant daily flow of minor slights, mishaps and disruptions they need to be seen within the life-death-new life framework, just as a major crisis is.

Despair or new life?

For humans each "death" event can basically lead to some level of despair or, alternatively, new life.

The better option is "new life." A key first step to ensuring that is the path followed is familiarising yourself with the evidence that it does and can happen.

The evidence is everywhere that many people are embittered and resentful about hurtful and tragic events they have been through.

Other people get through some of the most traumatic and appalling events and work hard to continue living a positive, contented, contributing life.

Make a private mental list (or even a written list if you can keep it safe and confidential) of family, friends and acquaintances who you think fall into each category. Which list would you currently put yourself in? Be honest. If it is "despair" at the moment that is okay. You do not need to pretend your spirituality is strong if it is not. Many people are in the same position, to some extent, at the start. The whole point of the Resurrection Mantra is to shift you into the other column as soon as we can.

Let us revisit the five "death" event examples we used above and now add some "new life" options.

1. Being ridiculed or attacked online

Death: Part of our privacy, self-confidence, public image and reputation dies. It is embarrassing and upsetting.

New life: Some friends come to our defence and those relationships are strengthened, we calmly and accurately defend ourselves and our positive profile is lifted, we decide to close our social media accounts and avoid the toxicity.

2. Locking the keys in the car

Death: Control over the vehicle dies. Part of our daily schedule dies as time is lost fixing the problem.

New life: Instead of rushing around, we are forced to sit and wait until the car is unlocked, a friendly stranger helps us and we enjoy the new encounter and goodwill, we learn a new skill such as how to unlock a car without the keys.

3. Separation or divorce

Death: A marriage dies. Love and respect dies. A whole list of dreams die – growing old together, enjoying the simplicity and efficiency of a happy family living together, providing the children with a unified, safe, secure environment.

New life: We seek out and develop new hobbies and experiences to avoid isolation, we make new friends outside the "married couple" world, we review our own life and its weaknesses and strengths as we assess what happened, we become less concerned about the views and opinions of others.

4. Marriage

Death: This is one many do not consider, but many marriages do go through difficult periods at the start because marriage represents the death of the single, independent life. One lifestyle has died and is replaced by another, quite different one. This can be a painful experience for many people and, to make sense of it and better handle it, the experience should be seen as a life-death-new life event. We die to the single life and rise to a new shared life. It can take time and involve physical, mental and spiritual adjustment.

New life: Life's projects are now shared with someone we love, we become less selfish and self-centred, we start a family, we work together to create a house and home, we have an intimate help-mate in times of difficulty.

5. Getting older

Death: The death of youthful energy, dreams and idealism. Death of the "trim, taut and terrific" look of our teens and twenties. The death of clear, unwrinkled skin. Death of a decent head of hair or its unblemished colour. Dying eyesight. Dying libido (e.g. impotence) and reproductive function (e.g. menopause).

New life: We develop more wisdom, our conversation matures, our career advances, we are taken more seriously in important situations.

These "new life" options are not magic and do not necessarily happen. They depend on choices made and your outlook on life – that is, the strength of your spirituality and the extent to which you have your Body, Mind and Spirit in balance. A long list of negative outcomes can also be made in a "despair" column if you follow that option.

Spend some time going through the list and, in each case, identify the possible life-death-new life dynamic. You will see the evidence for this life pattern all around you. Once familiar with these examples your knowledge changes forever. However, this theoretical understanding is only a first step. The next step is to internalise the pattern as part of your personality, to make it an organising principle of your life.

Understanding and internalising this life-death-new life cycle is true enlightenment.

It is about building up spiritual values – no one can give you those. You have to be prepared, in your solitude, for life's malevolence and loss. Internalisation of the life-death-new life truth about life is necessary. Evidence-based spiritual exercises, such as the Resurrection Mantra, will help you with that internalisation process.

Conclusion

We have familiarised ourselves with the death and resurrection of Jesus Christ, the role of suffering in defining life and the overwhelming evidence for the life-death-new life pattern. We are now ready to discuss actually using the Resurrection Mantra.

Some thoughts on serious evil and tragedy

What about really serious evil and horrifying tragedy? It is a fair question.

At the extreme end of the scale there are some events that the rest of us wonder how people ever get through. Examples include death of a child, murder and child abduction. These extreme events are still common enough to cause considerable anxiety across society.

These are the types of events that plunge many of the lives affected into an especially dark place. However, around the world it is also clear that many people do get through somehow and build meaning and new life out of the wreckage.

The evidence is again all around us that people do get through seriously horrendous events, the type of events that leave the rest of us just looking on in shock.

The challenge is the same as in every other crisis. How to work through the trauma to avoid despair. The amazing thing is we see people doing it all the time. For example, families:

- getting involved in victims support;
- engaging in greater community engagement to help others;
- campaigning for legal and services reform;
- setting up education and awareness programs: and

- raising money for childhood diseases research in the name of their lost child.

Even in the darkest of scenarios people can and do find new life. We observe people survive extreme trauma all the time.

The death of Jesus Christ was itself one such extreme, unjust scenario.

Exercises: The proof in your own life

To reinforce this evidence for the life-death-new life pattern, it is useful to describe examples from your own life.

Developing this type of mental imagery is useful. It stimulates your imagination, so you can better envision the potential out of suffering rather than the darkness.

Importantly, once you see the life-death-new life pattern in your own life, it then becomes very hard to "un-see" it.

1. Write about your past – identify a number of setbacks or crises you have already been through in life and look for evidence of the life-death-new life pattern or, if you are still troubled by the event, look for the reasons why new life has not emerged yet and what type of new life is possible out of the experience.

On the computer or in a journal or diary, these headers might help:

- Name the event:
- Describe or list your painful experiences/emotions/feelings at the time:
- Describe or list the new, good things emerging from the event or experience:

2. Write about your present – identify some difficult situations you are currently dealing with and describe them within the life-death-new life pattern.

On the computer or in a journal or diary, these headers might help:

- Name the event:
- Describe or list what painful experiences/emotions/feelings you are going through:
- Describe or list the new, good things emerging or you think could emerge from this event or experience:

3. Write about your future – identify a possible crisis you could face in the future, or something you dread might happen to you, and describe how the event might play out, hurt or traumatise you and then become a source of new meaning and action.

On the computer or in a journal or diary, these headers might help:

- Name the event:
- Describe or list what you fear about this and what painful experiences/emotions/feelings you would expect to go through:
- Describe or list how you might build new life out of the trauma:

Chapter Eight

The Resurrection Mantra and mantra exercises

HAVING seen the overwhelming evidence for the life-death-new life pattern, which allows us to overcome adversity and suffering and continue living a positive, meaningful life, it is time to start using the Resurrection Mantra exercise so you can absorb, internalise and really believe this important truth about life.

What is a Mantra exercise?

The term now has a number of meanings in general conversation.

For our purposes, a mantra is a simple spiritual exercise involving a word or phrase that is repeated to calm or focus the mind to ultimately achieve the desired spiritual purpose.

The process of repeating the word or phrase helps with concentration when meditating on the idea described by the word or phrase. This can deliver strong psychological and spiritual growth, if based on reality and done regularly, because it closes down distractions and focuses you on embedding the mantra phrase's central idea in your thinking and disposition.

What is the Resurrection Mantra?

The Resurrection Mantra is a mantra exercise based on a short phrase, or variations of that phrase, which, through repetition in a meditative setting or mood, links you to the dramatic and powerful story of the death and resurrection of Jesus Christ. It integrates the story's life-death-new life pattern of resilience and hope into your thinking and disposition.

Understanding and internalising this life-death-new life pattern, condensed or summarized in the words of the mantra phrase, is true enlightenment.

The basic Resurrection Mantra phrase is:

Jesus, with you I will die and rise again.

Shorter variants include:

I will die and rise again

With Jesus I will die and rise again

Getting started

The sooner you start the Resurrection Mantra the better. It does not matter if your life is going along well or whether you are experiencing difficulty in your life when you start.

In fact, starting while you do not feel any pressing need in your life is an ideal time to change your thinking and build your spiritual strength for the next time your life does hit a hurdle or experience a setback or tragedy.

On the other hand, if you are dealing with anguish right now it is all the more reason to get started. Starting while you are struggling with some form of suffering or pain will help you rethink your attitude to the suffering and start the process of emerging from the negative grip it might have on your life.

The point is, get started and as soon as possible. It is about building up spiritual values – no one can give you those. You have to be prepared yourself for life's malevolence and loss. A realistic internalisation of the life-death-new life pattern is necessary. The care of others plus this internal resilience will help get you through. You cannot just rely on others or external props.

Further delay risks despair or what the United States psychologist and expert on positive psychology, Martin Seligman, called learned helplessness.

This is when an animal or person feels so brow beaten or overwhelmed that they accept they have lost control and thus give up trying, even as changing circumstances offer a method of relief from the said situation. Such an organism is said to have acquired learned helplessness.

You do not want to let this happen or, if it has already happened to some extent, to continue. Seligman observed that experience in controlling trauma can protect organisms from the helplessness caused by inescapable trauma. What he called "behavioural immunisation" provides an easy and effective means of preventing learned helplessness.

This is similar to my experience with the Resurrection Mantra. It is an easy and effective form of behavioural immunisation.

What to do

In simple terms the idea is to repeat the mantra phrase for a set number of times or for a set period of time at least once a day.

The idea is to, firstly, calm the mind, then retrain the mind and, finally, to internalise the truth so that it is increasingly integrated into your personality.

The ultimate goal is for the truth to be both known and freely embraced, not just known.

The ritual and repetition of the mantra exercise create rhythm, and drill-in instinctive responses to life. The more often you repeat the mantra phrase the deeper is the appreciation of its mystery. You savour the mystery. Your understanding of it becomes habitual, not just intellectual.

Where and how to do it

You can do it anywhere you feel comfortable and can relax, with few direct distractions.

You can do it while walking, jogging or exercising at the fitness centre. You can do it on the train or bus. Lying in bed at night before you go to sleep is a good time. That is my favourite time to do the main daily exercise.

It is not about complicated meditation systems. I personally find many recommended meditation positions – straight back, eyes closed, etc. - to be too intense and uncomfortable. If they work for you then use them, but do not feel bound by that type of rigour.

In short, wherever you feel comfortable then do it. However, what is essential is to devote some time each day to making our mind introspective, to strengthen our powers of perception.

Find the setting that suits you and then, at least once a day, recite the mantra phrase at least 100 times at one session. That is a four to five minute session. You can do more if you like. Everyone is different and there are no rigid rules about how long your main daily session should take. If you need a higher count or a longer time to calm your body and mind down and get into a meditative state then do more. The more experienced you get the more time you will probably want to spend, but, to get started, four to five minutes per day – at least 100 phrase recitations – is a good minimum target.

It is not just about relaxation and stress therapy, as useful as they can be. We do need to relax and destress at times. One of the best ways to destress is to get a good, drug-free night's sleep. This mantra exercise does help with that, but it is ultimately about developing the deeper insight into life expressed in the words of the mantra phrase. This requires a daily commitment, especially at the start.

Counting or prayer beads, like Catholic Rosary beads or a prayer rope, are also recommended as a way of keeping you focused and also keeping some sort of count. Catholic Rosary beads are easy enough to get and can be used for any type of mantra exercise like this, not just reciting the Catholic Rosary. Other types of counting beads also exist if you can get access to them.

Do not rush the words. Recite them in your mind at a moderate pace. At nine words, the phrase "Jesus, with you I will die and rise again" should take about three seconds to speak, so 2.5 to three seconds is the ideal pace when reciting mentally.

Starting off with a suitable image in your mind, from the death and resurrection of Jesus Christ, is a good way to remove any distractions and worries and to focus your thinking on the exercise getting underway.

Lying in bed at the end of the day, with a set of counting beads, reciting the Resurrection Mantra, with an image of the crucifix in your mind's eye, is an excellent way to calm the mind and slide into a good night's sleep. On the inside it will also be toning those spiritual muscles, strengthening you to better confront life's challenges.

Once you have established that main daily session as part of your routine, then you can also do mini-sessions at any other time of the day that suits or might require the calming impact of the mantra. Little bursts of five or ten phrase recitations throughout the day can significantly improve your day and keep you positive and content.

It might seem hard to believe, but the basic exercise is as simple as that.

Be reassured, excessive complexity is not essential to strengthening your inner self. The KIS – Keep It Simple – principle applies here as it does to so many things in life.

However, how the Resurrection Mantra fits into an integrated life requires a bit more discussion.

Let us have a closer look at what is happening and how it interacts with and assists the rest of your life, especially when you are experiencing suffering and pain.

Calming the mind

One of the most immediate benefits of this exercise is to help calm the mind. As the recitation count climbs other thoughts and distractions should decrease and any associated worries also decrease in intensity.

In that sense a mantra is similar to other mental counting exercises, like counting sheep to try and get to sleep or "taking a deep breath and counting to ten" to avoid lashing out in anger.

The difference is that the mantra, if the phrase points to a life truth as the Resurrection Mantra does, is higher quality and simultaneously links your thinking and attitude to the truth summarised in the mantra phrase.

Retraining the mind

As we have discussed in Chapter Five, humans are a unity of Body, Mind, and Spirit.

Just as poor eating habits are bad for our bodies, wrong thinking or poorly formed ideas can hold us back and, at times, even be a dangerous and destructive force in our lives.

A mantra like the Resurrection Mantra is ultimately a spiritual exercise, but insofar as its phrase also summarises an important life truth, such as the life-death-new life pattern, it helps retrain the mind to implant the idea in the memory.

This is a simple idea, which we are familiar with from things like learning a poem or the multiplication table. Most people can quickly recall that six times six equals 36, because at some point in their life they repeated the idea enough times to imprint it in the brain or "learn it off by heart."

It is the same with the Resurrection Mantra. Through repetition we "learn off by heart" the life-death-new life pattern.

We have seen the evidence for this pattern, so we now commit it to memory. You purify your thoughts and get rid of any muddled or incorrect ideas you have about how life really is. In so doing, your intellectual understanding of the world and life is fundamentally changed. You can never look at life the same way again.

Having memorised the truth of the Resurrection Mantra phrase, it does not yet mean you can fully live with your new understanding, but your mind is now forever tugging at you with the truth. You have been intellectually "immunised" and, like antibodies fighting off bacteria and viruses, your mind is constantly fighting back. It has become a mental habit.

This changed knowledge of how life works – the engraving or imprinting of it on the mind - is an essential first step, which we then need to internalise – engrave or imprint it on the "heart" (spirit).

The repetitive reciting of the Resurrection Mantra phrase retrains the mind in another way, which is also an essential early step. It helps us get into the habit of excluding non-essential thoughts and distractions from our mind. We will discuss the importance of this in a little more detail in the next section.

Internalising the truth

While the Resurrection Mantra does calm and retrain the mind, as a mantra it is first-and-foremost a spiritual exercise based on meditation.

Do not let that word put you off. As discussed above in the section on "Where and how to do it," we are not talking about some complicated, esoteric idea or process. We are not talking about convoluted systems of posture, chanting and mysticism.

It does require commitment, regularity and some self-control, but it is simple enough.

Through this simple meditation we move from the mind to the "heart." Once you have moved through calming and retraining the mind, you will notice yourself becoming more collected, serene, centered. That indicates you are going deeper into yourself. You are meditating. The truth of life's death-resurrection pattern is moving from an intellectual concept to a lived, experienced phenomenon. The words are not just something we say or know, but they are part of who we are and how we approach life. The mental habit has become an internal or lived habit.

Essential to this is the habit of excluding non-essential thoughts and distractions from your mind. The repetitive reciting of the Resurrection Mantra phrase will achieve this, but it will not necessarily happen immediately. This is why a daily commitment to the Resurrection Mantra exercise is strongly recommended, especially at the beginning.

Meditation and concentration

The point is, meditation is inseparable from concentration. Effective meditation on the resurrection truth means concentrating on it.

Concentration means holding the mind to one point. In everyday life we concentrate when we are doing something important or precise. We focus intently on that one issue or task. At that point we are trying to govern all our thoughts, ignore distractions, and hold our mind steadily on the object of our concentration.

It can be hard to concentrate. Our mind is claimed and distracted by many things. Do no force it or get upset if it is not working immediately. Everyone has the same experience at first. As a beginner to the mantra exercise your mind is more than likely in constant struggle. It will not obey or do what you want it to do. Eventually you must make it obey and you will. However, it does involve some effort and persistence. It takes time for this mantra to work, so let it have that time.

Nevertheless, concentration is eventually essential when reciting the mantra phrase or prayer. Focus your mind on the words and images involved and keep bringing yourself back to them, when worries and other unrelated thoughts flow back into the mind.

Just keep gently refocusing yourself. Each time your mind wanders, stop yourself, concentrate again and gently keep bringing your mind and body back to the words and imagery. It is a spiritual exercise, not a mental or intellectual exercise, even though mental and intellectual forces are part of it.

The key thing is to not stress about this problem. Do not put too much pressure on your body or mind. That will only make things worse. Just accept that internal and external distractions are normal, especially at the start. Be gentle with yourself and keep reminding yourself that it takes a little while to build good concentration practices. It cannot be emphasised enough that it is a gradual process, so try not to be impatient and rush things. Just keep moving steadily forward each day and your powers of concentration will increasingly improve.

The objective is to eliminate disturbances from the mind and, with practice and repetition, you will get better at it. Your mind becomes stronger and is better able to shut out whatever disturbs it – external sounds and images, all external sense perceptions, internal thoughts, desires and worries. Through patience and perseverance, rather than mental brute force, you will have developed the habit of shutting out all non-essential thoughts and distractions.

When you are struggling to concentrate, there cannot be effective meditation, because meditation is a state of collectiveness or unity of thought. The effectiveness of your meditation depends on the intensity of your concentration. This is because concentration always gives power. It is about collecting your forces.

This intensity is not a mental stress, but a peaceful relaxed state, free of distraction and focused on the truth contained in the mantra phrase. If your mind is stressed rather than relaxed, albeit disciplined and focused, then you are using your mental processes to try and rush things. Coming back to focus, when distracted, should be a gentle step, not something that gives you a headache.

In other words, don't let the perfect be the enemy of the good. This mantra will not get you to a peaceful place immediately, but it will. Persist and you will reap the benefits.

As your meditation matures your consciousness is extending. Just as learning increases your knowledge, meditation expands your consciousness. Life's horizons are significantly broadened. Through the Resurrection Mantra your individual consciousness merges, through meditation on the death and resurrection of Jesus Christ, with the universal life-death-new life pattern.

It might sound like a grand idea, but it is not. It is straightforward enough. The simple truth summarised in the Resurrection Mantra phrase demystifies a lot of words and talk about life and its challenges.

A note for Christians

For the Christian it also demystifies a lot of spirituality and theology. God does not work in mysterious ways. His ways are clear – resurrection out of death; new life out of death experiences. Through the death and resurrection of his Son, Jesus Christ, God reveals the truth that hope is justified in a flawed, free creation, defined by the inevitable suffering caused by people's flawed, free choices.

Through Jesus Christ, God says that, without interfering with our freedom, he can do nothing about the inevitability of suffering. But, through Jesus Christ he also says: *I do understand. There is new life if you choose it and look for it.*

Yes, Jesus Christ was a teacher and talked a lot about how to live life and treat others: Love one another, be merciful, be a Good Samaritan.

That is, live the virtuous life. But, it will never be enough. There will never be utopia, because of the flawed nature of things. In that sense Christianity is not a social program.

The real message of Christianity is that life is fallen and defective, but Jesus Christ has beaten that. His resurrection defeats death and your sharing in it will help you defeat the death moments in your life. No matter how often you fail, fall or are hurt, there will be new life. Get back up and keep going in search of that new life. The Resurrection Mantra can give you the spiritual strength and confidence to do that.

It helps you internalise the central Christian event – the death and resurrection of Jesus Christ:

> *The Kingdom of God does not come in such a way as to be seen. No one will say 'look here it is', or 'there it is' because the Kingdom of God is within you.*
> Luke 17:20-21

The Christian faith brings healing and harmonising power into lives broken by suffering, disillusioned by experience, and sunk in despair. Psychological factors account for many breakdowns. Bodily treatment is essential where physical disorder exists.

However, the integration and healing of the whole person requires much more, based on a fuller diagnosis of the mind and spirit. The problem may be due to moral challenges, a troubled conscience, fears that need to be brought into the open, faced and dealt with, and similar factors. However, the Christian believes that only a whole new orientation to life itself, based on faith in the goodness of God, will paralyse these fears and weaknesses, and release joy and confidence in a disorganised life.

Chapter Nine

The Resurrection Mantra and life

HAVING outlined how to do the Resurrection Mantra exercise, let us now discuss a number of ways that it can interact with and assist the rest of your life, especially when you are experiencing suffering and pain.

Your general outlook on life

In retraining your brain to understand and recognise the life-death-new-life pattern and internalising it into your temperament and outlook on life, the Resurrection Mantra can help you avoid a descent into negativity and give you a reasonable optimism about life.

It can help develop a hopeful personality, with resilience and creative/problem solving capacity in challenging situations. You will be less apt to make the mistakes caused by bitterness and despair and, as a result, less time is wasted undoing any damage done.

You can also become more tolerant, loving, and enduring and less panicky, reactive and defensive. Over time you become practiced at dealing with anxiety and fear, including the fear of failure.

Your life will be a lot more enjoyable and satisfying if you have a realistic optimism.

This is not about wishful thinking. It does not deny the reality of suffering, evil or tragedy. It is about developing and nurturing a temperament and outlook that gives you the ability to act, function and keep your equilibrium irrespective of what life throws at you.

Gratitude, as opposed to resentment, is a feature of this. You should find yourself being more thankful for what you have. You increasingly focus on the things that are working, which are signs of new life, rather than what is not working or has gone wrong.

1. Children and young people

Given this potential impact on how you view life, it is the type of spiritual exercise that will significantly benefit children.

I suspect Catholic and other denominational schools are more likely to adopt this idea than public or government schools, but spiritual exercises like this are an important part of preparing children for life, especially the challenges of adult life.

We might have taught our children how to write, add up or understand chemistry. Have we taught them how to get through losing a job, business betrayal or losing a child without descending into a life of despair?

The sooner we can get young people to see and internalise the life-death-new life pattern of life the more resilient and positive they will be. The younger they are when this process starts, with age appropriate examples and simulations, the better.

2. Being more useful to others

Once the life-death-new life truth governs your outlook on life, it will affect how you interact with others, especially when they are going through episodes of suffering and pain.

You should find the suffering of others, no matter how severe, less intimidating or scary, just as you find it less threatening in your own life.

If your personality or consciousness has a bias towards the hope in life, then you can be the basis of hope for people you care about who are in a crisis. You will be able to provide more meaningful and consistent assistance and be a better friend or support person, because you have a clearer understanding of the forces at work.

This is not about preaching or providing gratuitous advice. It is about understanding what the ultimate outcome can be – some form of new life – if the situation is handled properly and the person is unobtrusively supported through the normal and natural grief they will experience.

You are also less likely to hurt other people. Most of the harm that we do to other people arises out of suffering and pain – usually when we are trying to avoid it, get revenge, or "get in first" in a conflict situation. In times of suffering and pain people will sometimes lash out at others, blame others or try to drag them down. In such situations it is despair, not hope, which is dominating the person's personality.

The day-to-day

Every day we face irritations and annoyances – little deaths if you like – and they can mount up over the day or week. They can also add up over time to give us a negative outlook on life and view of other people.

The community – whether it is the workplace, the family or the school - is always at risk of disruption by individual conflicts and differences of opinion and worldview. Personal emotion and need is always swirling around inside us. The best of intentions are easily disrupted or distracted by the individual's personal internal war.

It is spirituality that best contains this internal war. The Resurrection Mantra can help you maintain your composure and contentment in the face of this constant daily flow of minor slights, mishaps and disruptions.

I have found it especially helpful in these micro-aggression situations.

Whenever a feeling of resentment, disappointment, jealousy or failure comes up try saying the mantra phrase a few times until it subsides. This helps refocus your thinking and feelings at the point the problem emerges.

If you are feeling nervous ahead of a meeting or personal encounter, mentally recite it a few times to calm things down and keep things in perspective. This can help with staying calm and not being reactive, which usually only makes things worse.

If you are feeling nervous, annoyed or bored in a meeting, do the same a few times to re-engage yourself in a positive way.

In these situations the Resurrection Mantra helps remind you there is really little or nothing to be nervous or reactive about. What real long-term harm can occur in these day-to-day situations? One way or another everything can lead somewhere good. It helps you get through the instant surge of emotion or desire, avoid becoming unsettled and focus on finding the opportunities that exist in the situation.

As for boredom, it is an important human experience, which drives so much internal aggravation. Learning to live with boredom is essential to contentment. When those moments of boredom arise and threaten your attentiveness and good mood, the Resurrection Mantra can help you resettle.

Using the Resurrection Mantra in these little situations or events of the day also helps you build up spiritual strength for any larger issues you might have to get through. You are regularly focusing yourself in a real life scenario, which means it is increasingly becoming a natural and instinctive part of your approach to life.

Loneliness

There is little argument around the world that loneliness is an escalating problem in many societies. It has been described as the health epidemic of our age. It is extremely stressful, can send you into a downward physical and psychological spiral and even be deadly.

In January 2018 the government of Great Britain appointed a Minister for Loneliness, in response to a commission of inquiry into the issue. The American Psychological Association has published on the problem too. Statistics being quoted in country after country around the world, for the incidence of loneliness, are disturbing.

There are sections of the population who face serious physical and mental health barriers to easily meeting and interacting with others. Community services such as home visitation, special social events and adopt-a-friend are definitely required in cases such as this. In some cases psychiatric and counselling interventions will be necessary.

However, the extent of the international problem now being described suggests there is a lot of unnecessary loneliness, which is being driven by individual reticence, loss of self-confidence and personal pessimism.

Many of the solutions being put forward also continue and even reinforce the body-mind imbalance and completely ignore this spiritual – outlook on life - dimension of loneliness.

Loneliness frequently arises out of life events involving loss. Long term loneliness can result from unresolved grief and the failure to accept that a previous world is lost and a new one has to be built.

For example, your wife or husband has died or separated from you. Loneliness will be a normal and natural part of the grief process. That is to be expected. However, if it goes on for too long, it suggests a failure to progress through the grief process to acceptance and new life. In the long run you need to do something else for company or you will be lonely.

The same can occur after retirement from work, having a baby or moving to a new town or city. The list of situations that can change or disrupt your relationships and social environment is long. They can either lead to new relationships (new life) or loneliness. The life-death-new life pattern still applies.

Community services and support can help achieve that new life, by facilitating contact with other people and the building of new friendships. As stated, professional services such as doctors and counsellors might also be necessary at times. These community and professional services can help with the Body and Mind dimensions of the issue.

In addition to that, you also have to be at peace with yourself and your own company and possess an outlook on life that integrates with those Body and Mind solutions.

An intimate partner who has died cannot be replaced. Even with new friends and a second marriage, that specific loss will always be with you in some way. You can only come to terms with that within yourself. It is a spiritual challenge resolved within the life-death-new life pattern.

In positively coming to terms with your new social situation you reduce the risk of long-term gloom and build up the creative mindset essential to re-engaging with others and the wider world.

Social isolation is one of those things that can quickly become learned helplessness. To avoid loneliness you need to avoid such a mindset at all costs.

This all means that a healthy spiritual life, nurtured by simple spiritual exercises, is essential to the ultimate defeat of loneliness. Your attitude and choices matter. Others can only do so much.

The Resurrection Mantra helps build the engaging, creative disposition necessary to, firstly, enjoying your own company when you are alone and, secondly, finding the new hobbies, activities and relationships that will enrich your life. It can also help you overcome the fear of rejection, meeting new people and reaching out to others.

The Resurrection Mantra will help you see rejection, as you move out of your isolation and back into the world, for what it is: A minor "death" event, a small pothole on the road to a new life.

Grief: Responding to loss or "death" experiences

The standard psychological or emotional response to loss or setback – a "death" event or experience - is grief. This is true, to a greater or lesser extent, for all such events. The intensity of the grief response depends on the magnitude of the event and the temperament of the sufferer.

The most common model used for understanding grief is the five-stage model described by the Swiss-United States psychiatrist, the late Dr Elisabeth Kübler-Ross, in her 1969 book *On Death and Dying*. This five-stage model is well documented in books and online.

It is strongly recommended that you familiarise yourself with the topic and its development and expansion since Elisabeth Kübler-Ross's watershed work. It is not complicated and will not take long.

This is because – as made clear at the start and throughout this booklet – the Resurrection Mantra is not about avoiding or denying the reality of grief, hurt or stress. That would be ridiculous and unrealistic; romantic nonsense and a denial of human nature. The Resurrection Mantra is about the reality of life, not denying the way life is.

In summary, Dr Kübler-Ross's five stages or phases of grief are:

> **1. Denial:** The shock phase when you first become aware of the loss or the pending loss. You cannot believe it. You refuse to believe it. It is a form of emotional numbness. The person who appears to be "coping well" as they prepare the funeral of a loved one is usually in this denial phase.
>
> **2. Anger:** Once the loss starts to sink in you resent it. You lash out at its unfairness or the person, people or object you think caused it.
>
> **3. Bargaining:** Once the loss sinks in you might also find yourself asking why? Or mentally negotiating to avoid or try and remove the reality of the situation.
>
> **4. Depression:** Once the reality really sinks in a sense of helplessness and inevitability consumes you and you become despondent. A sense of emptiness drains your motivation. This is reactive depression and perfectly normal. In fact, it would be quite strange if, after a major loss or crisis, you did not feel depressed about it at some point.
>
> **5. Acceptance:** The intensity of these anger, bargaining and depression feelings starts to recede. You might not be happy about it, but you increasingly find yourself accepting the reality of the situation and recognising that the new circumstances are a permanent reality.

In some respects the term "stage" is misleading. You do not necessarily go through these emotions in order. Nor do you necessarily go through all of them and you will often find yourself jumping backwards and forwards between them. For example, even if you have got to the point of acceptance of what happened, you will still have the occasional bad day, when feelings of sadness come back.

The so-called "stages" are really just psychological categories, which help us understand what we are experiencing and that those experiences are a normal and natural part of grief.

The point is, there is no avoiding the suffering of grief – the anger, depression, pleading. The Resurrection Mantra will be better integrated into your life if you understand what is happening when you have these normal feelings.

There was nothing romantic about the execution of Jesus Christ. The "death" or "crucifixion" stage is right in the middle of the life-death-new life pattern. Neither is the Resurrection Mantra about being reckless or nonchalant – don't worry, everything will be okay in the end - in the face of loss and trauma. Such events are serious and tragic and should be treated respectfully as such.

However, it is about whether you let loss and trauma destroy you. In such circumstances you are at a cross roads – you can choose despair or hope.

Getting to the acceptance point of the grief process is not necessarily the same thing as the "new life" we are describing in the Resurrection Mantra. Acceptance can be an optimistic emergence from the swirl of anger, bargaining and depression or it can be a drift into a begrudging, disillusioned existence.

The Resurrection Mantra provides the spiritual support for responsible action, made possible by a sense of hope. You do not erase the pain. You just start to keep it in perspective and manage it, as you transition into some form of new life. You avoid the despair option.

Having said that, it is timely to remember that spirituality is just one of the three pillars of an integrated life. It works with the Body and Mind.

Relying only on spirituality, especially in a serious crisis or when your life is badly disrupted, would be just as much a mistake as the current tendency to only rely on Body and Mind solutions.

In a crisis you will need the help of others. You might even need professional help such as general medical care, medication, psychiatric assistance, financial help, emergency accommodation, a rehabilitation program and the list goes on.

You should never hesitate to seek help in a crisis and when you find yourself in an emotionally dark place as a result of loss or trauma. This is especially true if the grief emotions are piercingly painful and/or you find yourself trapped in chronic grief, when it is taking far too long to get to some point of acceptance, or experiencing the symptoms of post-traumatic stress disorder (PTSD). Time does not always heal and, if your suffering drags on, then get professional advice and help.

To make best use of this Body and Mind support and assistance you also need the spiritual or "inner" resources and positive orientation of "new life" thinking. You can help heal your memories with the Resurrection Mantra as it integrates your spirituality into your psychological and physical healing processes.

Chapter Ten

The Resurrection Mantra in eight easy steps

1. Accept your spiritual dimension and commit to taking care of it.

Mind, Body, Spirit means that our well-being comes from physical health, but also from mental health and spiritual health. To be "healthy," we must pay attention to all three aspects of our nature - Body, Mind and Spirit.

2. Accept the essential rhythm or pattern of life: Life- death-new life.

   Life: While nothing is ever perfect, your life is flowing relatively smoothly.

   Death: A setback or crisis (a death event) disrupts that flow and causes upset.

   New life: The setback or crisis forces some changes and a re-evaluation, leading to a new direction, new skills or new opportunities

3. Familiarise yourself with the Easter story details: The death and resurrection of Jesus Christ.

   Life: Jesus Christ is popular with the people and well received by the general public as he enters Jerusalem

   Death: The betrayal, arrest, trial and execution of Jesus Christ.

   New Life: The resurrection of Jesus Christ and the transformation and re-invigoration of his supporters.

4. Describe a few life-death- new life experiences you have already been through in life - describe each phase separately. On the computer or in a journal or diary, these headers might help:

- Name the event:
- Describe or list your painful experiences/emotions/feelings at the time:
- Describe or list the new, good things emerging from the event or experience:

5. Identify in your own life any death experiences that have not led to new life, but resentment or despondency instead. Try and imagine where the new life might be found in those experiences – again describe each phase separately.

6. Memorise the Resurrection Mantra phrase:

Jesus, with you I will die and rise again

7. Familiarise yourself with art work depicting the death of Jesus Christ, to assist your imagination to focus when reciting the mantra phrase.

8. Start reciting the Resurrection Mantra phrase at least 100 times a day (four to five minutes) in one session – count them out with beads (such as Catholic Rosary beads) if necessary. Then increase the count and time to suit yourself, but always do at least 100 per day. Recite at other times of the day if you can.

If you are in a crisis recite as often as necessary to calm the mind and thoughts and assist with things like sleep.

Yes, it is as simple as that. So, why not get started?

Postscript

Going a little deeper
John Cassian & Abbot Isaac

AS OUTLINED in the Introduction, the Resurrection Mantra is a personally developed and tested exercise that has worked for me, which might also work for you. That's basically it. I developed and trialled it over the last 10 to 15 years, largely unassisted except for my rudimentary background knowledge of mantras, meditation and theology, acquired over the course of my 60 years.

As I started to share it with a select group around the world, during the preparation of this book, I was taken completely by surprise when a leading historian at the University of Chicago, Professor Rachel Fulton Brown, who specialises in the medieval period and its spirituality, replied with the following:

> It occurs to me that you are a latter day Abbot Isaac. Are you familiar with John Cassian's "Conferences," talking with the Desert Fathers in Egypt? Your description of the mantra fits well with what Abbott Isaac describes as having a formula for prayer. He describes some of the same effects as you do, as well as giving reasons for having a set phrase to use to anchor one's understanding.

After reading the material referred to, her suggestion that "it might be interesting to include some mention of Cassian" was taken up enthusiastically. Here it is.

John Cassian was a Christian monk who lived in the fourth and fifth centuries. His writings and spiritual traditions played a big role in the development of Western Europe. He wrote a major, influential work on monastic life, but the work of most interest here is his *Conferences of the Egyptian Monks,* which recorded the wisdom of the Egyptian Christian hermits, the Desert Fathers, in the form of dialogues by famous abbots.

One such luminary was Abbot Isaac, introduced to me by Professor Fulton Brown, whose ideas are described in Conferences 9 and 10 of this literary and spiritual classic. Isaac does echo many Resurrection Mantra themes.

He describes, in the style of the day, the value of a truthful, meaningful phrase (pious formula was his phrase) being constantly with you, as an "impregnable wall" against setbacks and evil – "helpful and useful to every one of us in whatever condition we may be."

Isaac also emphasises the importance of evidence, which means the words are situated in our own lived experience. When this is achieved the reciter:

> *...will utter them (the phrase words) with the deepest emotion of heart not as if they were the compositions of the Psalmist, but rather as if they were his own utterances and his very own prayer; and will certainly take them as aimed at himself, and will recognise that their words were not only fulfilled formerly by or in the person of the prophet, but that they are fulfilled and carried out daily in his own case. For then the Holy Scriptures lie open to us with greater clearness and as it were their very veins and marrow are exposed, when our experience not only perceives but actually anticipates their meaning, and the sense of the words is revealed to us not by an exposition of them but by practical proof ... and so instructed by our feelings as our teachers we lay hold of it as something not merely heard but actually seen, and, as if it were not committed to memory, but implanted in the very nature of things, we are affected from the very bottom of the heart, so that we get at its meaning not by reading the text but by experience anticipating it.*

He affirms the need to remove distractions and the burdens of the day as you meditate/pray:

> *And so the mind, as it is always light and wandering, is distracted even in time of service by all sorts of things ... it is thinking about something that has to be done, or remembering*

> *something that has been done. And in this way it takes in and rejects nothing in a disciplined and proper way, and seems to be driven about by random incursions, without the power either of retaining what it likes or lingering over it. It is then well for us before everything else to know how we can properly perform these spiritual offices, and keep firm hold of this particular verse which you have given us as a formula, so that the rise and fall of our feelings may not be in a state of fluctuation from their own lightness, but may lie under our own control.*

Once in the routine you can recite the phrase anywhere, anytime (pray without ceasing):

> *We must then ceaselessly and continuously pour forth the prayer of this verse, in adversity that we may be delivered, in prosperity that we may be preserved and not puffed up. Let the thought of this verse, I tell you, be conned over in your breast without ceasing. Whatever work you are doing, or office you are holding, or journey you are going, do not cease to chant this. When you are going to bed, or eating, and in the last necessities of nature, think on this. This thought in your heart may be to you a saving formula, and not only keep you unharmed by all attacks of devils, but also purify you from all faults and earthly stains, and lead you to that invisible and celestial contemplation, and carry you on to that ineffable glow of prayer, of which so few have any experience. Let sleep come upon you still considering this verse, till having been moulded by the constant use of it, you grow accustomed to repeat it even in your sleep. When you wake let it be the first thing to come into your mind, let it anticipate all your waking thoughts, let it when you rise from your bed send you down on your knees, and thence send you forth to all your work and business, and let it follow you about all day long.*

So, the Resurrection Mantra exercise is similar to ancient and tested models of spiritual exercise/prayer, which were discussed and recommended by two of the greatest spiritual thinkers and practitioners of history – John Cassian and the Desert Father, Abbot Isaac.

John Cassian's two *Conferences of Abbot Isaac* are recommended reading for anyone who wants a deeper understanding of spiritual exercises such as the Resurrection Mantra.

Post postscript

The bodily resurrection of Jesus Christ
A few thoughts for people of faith

FOR CHRISTIANS the death and resurrection of Jesus Christ is much more than an example of how suffering and pain can lead to new life in the here and now. The resurrection is a real historical event, which involved a dead Jesus Christ leaving his tomb with some sort of transformed new body. It points the way to what happens to a faithful person when they actually die, not just suffer before death. There is eternal life beyond our physical bodies and existence in this life or this universe.

Plenty has been written about this by theologians, scientists and archaeologists. This book is not about repeating that. It can be easily accessed. However, something should be said about the tendency of some to scoff at these beliefs on the basis of so-called science or the idea that "we know better nowadays."

What you are usually dealing with in these situations is an out-of-date person trapped in the classical physics of the mechanical universe. This became popular a few hundred years ago and a group of people fell for the arrogant and ridiculous worship of such simple science as a source of meaning.

For them, and they aggressively tried to get the idea accepted across society, the world was no longer mysterious and wondrous, but instead resembled some kind of neat and tidy machine, like a well-crafted clock.

This world view and the associated intellectual arrogance were blown to smithereens in the first few decades of the 20th century. Classical physics is basically dead, except in so far as it is useful for things like engineering.

Quantum physics, with some help from Einstein's Relativity, changed everything. It shattered the mechanical world view. The so-called Enlightenment was a house of cards.

As one of the physicists caught up in it all, George Gamow, said in his book "Thirty Years That Shook Physics: The Story of Quantum Theory":

> *The opening of the twentieth century heralded an unprecedented era of turnover and re-evaluation of the classical theory that had governed Physics since pre-Newtonian times.*

It was indeed a full-scale scientific revolution, the likes of which we have never seen before. The problem is, the 20th century was then so disrupted by economic trauma and war, and the ideas and discoveries were so counter-intuitive, that its true import for wider culture was largely buried. However, many, including the quantum physicists themselves, understood its profound, potential cultural implications during the 1920s and 1930s and the general public were regularly reading about it in their daily newspapers. Philosophy and religion were back in play, for a while at least.

But, all consuming distractions like World War II basically brought that wider public discussion to an end. It is also true that most people struggle to grasp its complexity. As the United States quantum physics expert, Leonard Susskind, has said (Is the Universe a Hologram, https://www.youtube.com/watch?v=iNgIl-qIklU):

> *It is hard to understand. Our neural wiring was not built for quantum mechanics. It was not built for higher dimensions. It was not built for thinking about curved space-time. It was built for classical physics. It was built for rocks and stones and all the ordinary objects and it was built for three-dimensional space. And that's not quite good enough for us to be able to visualize and internalize the ideas of quantum mechanics and general relativity and so forth. ...that can be extremely frustrating when trying to explain to the outside world. The outside world, by and large, has not had that experience of going through the rewiring process of converting their minds into something that can deal with five dimensions, 10 dimensions, or the quantum mechanical uncertainty principle or whatever it happens to be. And so the best we can do is to use analogies, metaphors.*

Metaphor? So quantum physics has brought science full circle, back to the world of religion and the story telling methods of Jesus Christ and other religious figures?

Where quantum physics challenges everything, including those who arrogantly just dismiss things like the resurrection of Jesus Christ, is that it basically tells us two things:

1. There is no such thing as objective material objects; and

2. Consciousness has to be fundamental.

Now, let's be clear. This new science does not prove the resurrection or anything else of that nature. But, it does shatter the arrogant certainty of those who think science is all you need and has killed off the spiritual. Through quantum physics we were again reminded of just how much we don't know, especially about the mystery of the universe and the atomic world. In fact, we were not even close. This new quantum world was nothing like what scientists had envisaged prior to its discovery.

In the world with "spooky" features and interactions (to paraphrase Einstein on quantum theory) now being discovered by the quantum physicists, the resurrection of Jesus is no big deal. Neither are the Christian multiverses called heaven, hell and purgatory. This was well summarised for a fascinated public, by one well-informed writer in Queensland, Australia, in the daily press in 1939 (Percival Watson, Brisbane *Sunday Mail*, 9 April 1939, p.6):

> *When Jesus was stretched upon the Cross men said, 'That is the end of Him.' But it was not. It was his true beginning. Had he not conquered death he would have been forgotten with the thousands of other nameless victims who were crucified in those times. Had he not manifested his resurrection body to his frightened disciples, who had forsaken him and fled, they would never have returned to become the fearless preachers and martyrs of the Christian faith. The Christian Church would never have come into being, nor would the sign of the Cross ever have eclipsed the glory of the Roman Eagles. The resurrection of Christ from the dead has become the central fact of human history, and the symbol of that fact is an empty tomb. The*

> *miraculous element is of course a stumbling-block to many. But objectors to this cannot be as dogmatic to-day as they used to be. The new physics has reset all our ideas about the inviolability of natural laws. Professor Whitehead* (Alfred North Whitehead, British mathematician and philosopher), *no mean authority, asserts that much of the past emphasis of science on such so-called laws was 'pure bluff.' And he goes on to say, 'Heaven only knows what nonsense may not tomorrow be demonstrated as truth.' Students of Relativity and the Quantum theory may well believe him.*

The quantum and relativity revolution also restored respect for imagination, intuition and other forms of human knowledge and experience. For those who truly understood it, it brought science back to a closer relationship with religion and spirituality.

As quantum physicist and renowned science writer, Lee Smolin, said in 2006 (The Trouble with Physics: The Rise of String Theory, the Fall of a Science and What Comes Next):

> *Whatever they have been called, there has never been a human society without science, politics, art, and religion.*

As for putting your money where your mouth is, in the late 1940s, not long before his death, the story emerged that the father of quantum physics, Max Planck, had become a Catholic. In 1937, though not a Catholic at the time, he also accepted a position on the Vatican's Pontifical Academy of Science.

Further reading

Claire Felter: *The U.S. Opioid Epidemic*, Council on Foreign Relations, 2019, https://www.cfr.org/backgrounder/us-opioid-epidemic

George Gamow: *Thirty Years That Shook Physics: The Story of Quantum Theory*, Dover Publications, New York, 1985.

John Cassian: *The Conferences of John Cassian*, Christian Classics Ethereal Library, ca. 360-ca. 435, http://www.ccel.org/ccel/cassian/conferences.html

Jordan Peterson: *On the Death and Resurrection: A Psychological View in Five Parts*, https://www.jordanbpeterson.com/transcripts/death-and-resurrection/

Julianne Holt-Lunstad: *Loneliness: A Growing Public Health Threat*, American Psychological Association, 2017 annual conference, Session 3328, https://www.apa.org/news/press/releases/2017/08/lonely-die

Lee Smolin: *The Trouble with Physics: The Rise of String Theory, the Fall of a Science and What Comes Next*, Penguin Books, London, 2006.

Leonard Susskind: *Is the Universe a Hologram*, https://www.youtube.com/watch?v=iNgIl-qIklU):

Martin E. P. Seligman: *Learned Helplessness*, Annu. Rev. Med. 1972.23:407-412. Downloaded from www.annualreviews.org, University of Pennsylvania.

Rachel Fulton Brown: *Mary and the Art of Prayer: The Hours of the Virgin in Medieval Christian Life and Thought*, Columbia University Press, New York, 2018.

Sue Dunlevy: *Why our use of antidepressants has soared*, News Corp Australia Network, 23 April 2019, https://www.couriermail.com.au/lifestyle/health/why-our-use-of-antidepressants-has-soared/news-story/1f7a0ce118be22c21195c00649699b08

Theresa May: *PM commits to government-wide drive to tackle loneliness*, UK Government, Prime Minister's Office press release, 17 January 2018, https://www.gov.uk/government/news/pm-commits-to-government-wide-drive-to-tackle-loneliness

www.ingramcontent.com/pod-product-compliance
Lightning Source LLC
Chambersburg PA
CBHW060406050426
42449CB00009B/1917